QUIET MOMENTS
Selected Verse From The British Isles

AN ANTHOLOGY

Compiled and Edited

by

Michael K. Moore

THE HILTON HOUSE HILTON HOUSE (Publishers) ANTHOLOGY SERIES

1997

This edition published in the UK in 1997 by Hilton House (Publishers), Hilton House, 39 Long John Hill, Norwich, Norfolk NR1 2JP.

All Rights Reserved.

No part of this publication may be reproduced, stored in a retrieval system, or transmitted in any form or by any means electronic, mechanical, photocopying, recording or otherwise, without the prior permission of the publishers, Hilton House.

ISBN 1-900824-20-5

Copyright:

© Poems: Individual authors
© Compilation and editing: M.K. Moore

Conditions of sale

This book is sold subject to the condition that it shall not, by way of trade or otherwise, be lent, resold, hired out, or otherwise circulated, without the publisher's prior consent, in any form of binding or cover other than that in which it is published and without a similar condition including this condition being imposed on the subsequent purchaser.

Printed by Catton Printing,
13-14 Roundtree Close, Norwich, Norfolk, NR7 8SX

CONTENTS

		Page
Contents		v
Dedication		xii
Foreword		xiii
Abel, Nina.	My Imagination	132
A.D.	Love Must Not Die	71
Ainge, Maxine.	Thoughts	168
Alder, Francis.	Responsibility	10
Alston, Fred.	Memories - Demolished Birthplace	29
Anderson, Pauline.	The Pebble On The Beach	12
Anderson, Ray.	Eventide	89
Aquilla.	A Roller Coaster Ride	143
Armitstead, Simon.	Harvest Time	80
Axe, Valerie.	Immortal Rose	94
Ball, Margaret.	Insomnia	162
Barrett, Pamela.	Beloved Grandaughter	68
Bennett, Helen D.	Somewhere In Between	21
Beck, Beverley.	Blue Bear - True Bear	97
Betts, Patti.	Requiem	69
Bevan, Elizabeth.	Pictures	98
Blake, Susan P.	Memories From Childhood	76
Blaney, David.	Thought For Today	144
Bluck, Jean L.	The May Tree	30
Blundell, Kim.	A Candle	127
	The Lesson	130
Bradley, Terence J.	The Dancers	172
Brant, Terri.	Halloween	181
Brint, Roger.	Thoughts Of The Night	54
Brooks, Marilyn.	Betrayed	99
Broom, Bridget A.	Scarecrows	187
Brown, Anne V.	Those Were The Days	95
Brown, Margaret T.	Driftwood	36
Bryant, Kevin.	The River Composers	79
Butterworth, Albert.	To The Mayfly	18
Butwell, Richard.	A Summer's Day	171
Canham, Thomas.	Envy	78
Chambers, Frances.	Memories And Dreams	177
Chappell, John M.	Leicester, Early Morning	15
Coleman, Joseph N.	The Magic Box	82
Compton, Amanda C.	Southampton Water	192
Cookson, Mary M.	The Wonder Of You	170

		Page
Cooper, Daisy.	With A Little Help	180
Cooper, Ronald V.	Nigella Hispania	83
Corkill, Joan.	The Inevitable Revelation	179
Costello, Irene.	Our Derbyshire Village	39
	A Country Warden	44
Cowley Guscott, E.	Some Things Will Fade	37
Cox, Doreen.	Snow	147
Crean, Tom.	Winter Magic	191
	Lavinia	193
Cullup, Janet.	The Thief Of Joy	20
Cumner, Wendy.	Expressions Of Reality	96
Cundell, Cecil B.	Smile Of A Child	101
Curwen, Reginald.	The Husband's Dream	56
Daulton, Mary.	What Am I?	90
Day, Yvette.	Someone To Take The Blame	167
Dart, Douglas.	Winter's Grip	100
Davis, Paul.	The Red Rose And The Lady	31
Davison, Louise.	Likes	80
Delaney, Frances G.	Imagination	153
Dempsey, William E.	Whisper	61
	When	64
Dennison, Brenda.	Mountain Stream	62
Dent, Christine M.	Birthright	102
Dent, Eleanor.	The Awakening	103
Dickson, Alan.	The Missed Goodbye	128
Diston, Barbara.	Spring	61
Docker, William.	Charity	146
Dolby, Simmone.	Summer	149
Douglas, Gwendoline J.	The Song Of The Whale	74
Drion, Mona.	Dear Song Thrush	125
Dyson, Beryl.	A Veiled Request	2
Eastwood, M.V.	Don't Set The Clouds Too Low	104
Emmens, Joan M.	Anybody There?	102
Evans, Pamela.	Telephone Lines	159
Evans, Patricia.	Dimpsy Time	94
Field, Karin B.	Claire	105
Fletcher, Nicholas.	The Swan	127
Fox, Doreen.	New Day!	77
Fudge, Amanda.	Remembrance	106
Futer, Donald.	Eventide	4
	Pause A Moment	126
Garradley, Bert.	Assisted Passage	35

		Page
Gauld, Michael P.	Once Upon A Winter	47
Gibson, Michelle.	January Sunday	22
Godfrey, Jack.	Dream	22
Gray, Gordon.	On Silent Wing	123
Greaves, Peter K.	Love's Ghost	48
Griffiths, John.	Field Of Dreams	135
	Tomorrow	185
Hadley, Brenda M.	The Lakes In Winter	107
Hamilton, May.	Love	122
Hardy, Audrey.	Letting Go	182
Harris, Tristan.	The Universe And I	161
Harrison, David.	In Loving Memory Of A Name	189
Haywood, Nick.	Autumn	2
Heatley, William G.	Spring	121
Hampton, Helen.	The Sun Of Man	151
Hensom, Inez M.	Our World	148
Heppleston, Paul.	The Island	25
Herdman, Alexandra.	Lights, Cameras, Action	133
Hicks, Jane W.	In Touch	108
Hicks, Neville.	Today Forgotten	129
Howe, Terence M.	Pagan Beaches	120
Hubbard, Donna.	Golden Wedding Anniversary	93
Hughes, June.	Winter Elm	185
Hulme, Lynne.	Seagull	70
Humphrey, Brian.	Song of Maymyo	1
Hutchinson, W.	Today and Tomorrow	3
James, Andy.	Poetry For People	63
Jaynes, Amanda.	Beauty-Triggered Chain Of Thought	119
Jemson, Joan.	Dreaming	169
Jennings, David L.	Snow Storm	23
John, June L.	The Garden	27
Johns, Reginald B.	To Have You Near	84
Johnson, Jackie.	Once Upon A Dream	188
Jones, Corwena A.	Spring	130
Jones, Helen.	Ice-Man	38
Jones, Joyce M.	A Passionate Yuppy To His Love	32
Jones, Valerie A.	My Special Rainbow	85
Judge, Gerald A.	Cycle Of The Seasons	184
	Silent Playground - Vale Of Tears	184
Kelsey, Irene.	Blessings	138
Kiley, Ronald.	A Poem For Samantha / The Tree	87
Kimm, Alene.	On Humber Bridge 5.00am	42

		Page
King, Carolyn.	Wild Oats	173
Kitson, William.	Sunrise	26
	Poems	27
Laithwaite, Beryl M.	That Moment	41
Langdon, Cyril J.	A Dream Come True	86
Lapham, Peter.	As Each Day	91
Larter, Freda.	On Being Me	172
Lee, George A.	Enlightened	135
Leonard, B.	Immortal Mortal	14
Lisle, Malcolm.	Goodbye Happy Jeanette	89
Livingstone, David.	Pondering	34
Longville, Lindsey.	Pollution	24
Lucas, Louise.	Searching Through Lies	118
Lunt, Geofrey.	Cloud Thoughts	33
Luxon, Marcia.	Judgement Day	193
Lynch, Michael K.	Make It Last	88
Macklam, Susan.	The School Of Frightened People	58
Macpherson, Patricia.	The Oak Tree	166
Malkin, Samantha.	Creature Comforts	92
Maling, Muriel J.	Beauty - Or The Beast	57
Maloney, Jean K.	Changing Scenes	73
Manning, Adrian.	Legacy	157
Mansell, Pearl.	The Seeds Of Thought	43
Martin, Margaret.	The Summer Rose	65
Marshall, Valerie.	The New Life	156
Marston, Jan.	Honeysuckle Scent	164
May, Joyce.	Market Day	13
McCann, Sharon.	Security	170
McClung, Joan.	Listening	137
	Forgotten Journey	138
McNeill, Muriel.	To Spring - A Confusion Of Thought	41
McKenzie, Glenn.	Dreamland	134
Messenger, Steve.	Electronic Evolution	190
Mitchell, Derrick.	Where And Why?	39
Moore, Joanna.	A Perfect Day	194
Moore, Michael K.	Breckland Wilds	117
	The Black-Hooded Crow	195
Morton, Janet.	A Summer's Day	158
Mountain, Mary I.	Accidental Gift	178
Moyle, Norma.	Spring Song	52
Murfet, Pauline A.	Dreams	93

		Page
Musson, Colin.	Winter	165
Nelson, Mary.	Flotsam	75
Newcombe, Lynda.	Puffins Sit Upon The Rocks	152
North, Nyari J.	The Rocking Horse	137
Nuttall, Peter.	The Sky	116
Osborne, Jean M.	Dearest Treasure	163
Overall, Sonia L.	The 13th Of October	155
Pearson, David C.	Frozen In Time	40
	Coniston Water In Winter	116
Pepperell, B.M.	Without You	5
Phelen, Sean.	Vagrant Memory	150
Priest, Glenys.	Despair	154
Pritchard, Gwyneth.	Solitude	115
Quinnell, David.	Autumn Days	133
Ray, Nicholas A.	Money	114
Richards, David.	The Poet	14
Richards, Sonia E.	Masquerade	7
Richardson, Linda.	Memories Of A Moment	186
Robinson, Sarah.	The Vision	144
	Rain Through A Window	164
Rolph, John.	Trees	55
Roscoe, Vivienne.	Sonnet: Drops Of Rain	160
Rose, Pauleen S.	The Longest Sleep Of All	51
Round, Jean L.	Just You And Me	44
Roy, Michael.	Invoy (Message)	196
Royal, Norman.	A Calming Breeze	72
Savage, Edna.	Spirit Friends	9
Service, J. Margaret.	A Multitude Of Sins	67
Settle, Maureen C.	Rape Fields At Tranby Rise	28
Shaw, Dawn.	Observation	113
Sheppard, Linda.	God's World	146
Slater, Win.	The Twilight Cat	53
Smith, Andrew.	Reflection	11
Solli, Maggi.	Healer	60
	Cardboard City	66
Squire, Iris M.	Ploughman	65
Starr, Fred.	One Moment In Time	191
Stevenson, Janet.	Why?	183
Stokes, Elizabeth.	Autumn Leaves	45
Styles, Tony.	Who Am I?	17
Sullivan, Patricia M.	Sea Sound	112

Page

Sygrave, Rosemary A.V.	Appreciating Autumn	131
Tasker-Poland, Robert.	Song Of The Silver Star	139
Terry, Andy.	Just Girls	175
Thomas, Gloria.	Caerphilly Of Yesterday	136
Thomas, William G.	To: Life's Child	124
Thornber, Paul J.	Last Act (For Ella, 1910-1996)	109
Tooze, Maureen.	Regrets	176
Tye, Dennis F.	The Forest	145
Walker, Thomas.	No Cobbles No Clogs	110
Walton, Minnie.	Cow Parsley - In Praise Of	50
Watson, Peter.	To A Stone Circle	49
West, Harry J.	Beyond The Stars	59
Wickens, Clair.	Deaf	81
Williams, Diane S.	Changing Winds	6
Wilkes, Kirsty-Anne.	Tim Henman	174
Wilkinson, Wyn.	A Flower In The Wilderness	16
Wilson, Sheila J.	Nicola's Baby	142
Winfield, Alison.	Today	156
	A Handful Of Colours	160
Winfield, Francis.	Shadowscape	19
Wiseman, R.L.	Sarah's Sonnet	28
Wood, Susan W.	Summer	8
Worsley, Noelle.	Addiction	140
Wright, Jennifer.	Incarnate	141
Yates, Jane.	Mortal Men	111
Young, Maggie.	Newtown	46
ABOUT HILTON HOUSE:	Publisher's Information	198

Cover Photograph:

The ancient stone circle at Castlerigg, near Keswick, Cumbria, with Blenthcathra (Saddleback) in the background.

DEDICATION

To my father, Stanley (Pony) Frederick Moore, who, in 1939, at the Suffolk Regiment Depot, Gibralter Barracks, Bury St. Edmunds, ran a mile in under four minutes during a regimental sports day. The record was not recognised by the AAA, as the race was not classed as an official event and instead, the honour of being the first man in the world to break the four minute mile, went to Britain's Roger Bannister on May 6th, 1954 - Fifteen years after Stanley Moore unofficially broke the record. Sadly, Sergeant Moore was severely wounded during the Second World War and was never able to run again.

Born, 1912. Helions Bumpstead, Essex.		Died, 1983. Bury St. Edmunds, Suffolk.

Stanley Frederick Moore

When Death takes someone you dearly love,
    the loss is permanent and clear;
And their closeness is only within the mind -
    and in old photographs held near.
But for me, my loss, though so very deep,
    is comforted by memories I share -
With faded prints ... and a clear image of self,
    in reflection of glass held near;
And, I know in heart, thro' Death's misty veil
    the dead can reach out and care;
For, whenever I look into a mirror's depths -
    I see my father - standing there!

MICHAEL K. MOORE,
Norwich, Norfolk.

FOREWORD

Poetry is a blend of personal creativity, inspiration and inner thought. It is a language of communication that is a gift which only a few possess. Not everyone is a poet and those that have the ability of using words and projecting their thoughts to others are very special.

The language of the mind can be projected in many ways: by word, by writing, by movement of the eyes, head or hands. It can be complicated, or simple and covers many styles.

Poetry has developed over thousands of years - from the first oral traditions of the wandering bard to the written verse that we know today. This written verse can be in the form of traditional rhythmic and rhyming poetry; lyrical poetry; descriptive poetry; contemporary poetry; and the avant-garde seeking acceptance (and recognition) from a modern readership.

Consequently, all the different types of poetry (and we have not listed them all) do not always appeal to everyone (many of whom have their own interpretation of what they consider to be poetry). With this in mind, the poems in this anthology have been selected to give a wide range of verse which, perhaps, will not appeal to some readers; but will be accepted by the more general readership.

Many of these poems were submitted for the *Hilton House National Open Competition of 1996* and the *Hilton House National Poet Of The Year competition of 1997.*

The poems vary greatly in style, metre and theme and we hope you enjoy reading them as much as we have during their selection and final publication.

Michael and Joyce Moore,
Hilton House.

SONG OF MAYMYO
Burma 1945

Secluded in a mountain range ...
In rural majesty -
There lies a land I once surveyed ...
Two thousand feet above the sea,
... A land once mentioned in the psalms ...
Where living water flowed,
And lakes so crystal clear, I swear
God's purpose plainly showed ...
... For there He took me by the hand
And showed me many fruits -
That grew beside the mountain streams
Amid the tender bamboo shoots ...

I sipped the water from the stream
And felt my pulses race -
My very soul became refreshed
Whilst in His sweet embrace ...
I stood beneath a sapphire sky -
And gloried in His touch ...
And to this day, no memory
Can stir my heart so much ...!
Secluded in a mountain range ...
There is a land I know -
A land where I once saw the Light ...
And heard the song of Maymyo ...!

RUSSELL HUMPHREY,
Watford, Hertfordshire.

AUTUMN

Birds are flying swiftly south,
Clashing with the black sky's mouth.
Neatly weaving through the air,
This sight is very, very rare.
Children step on golden leaves,
Leaves that parted from sleeping trees.
All the dew like silver glitter,
Lays upon the ground like litter.
Rain is falling heavily and fast,
Showing signs that Summer has past.

NICK HAYWARD,
Wetheral, Carlisle.

A VEILED REQUEST

One wonders, will the spirit rest,
When it has sped away,
As body lies within the chest
To end in death's decay?
Or will it roam among the flowers
Or glide beneath the trees,
Need shelter from the heavenly showers
Or be carried on a breeze,
Haunt places one has seen and loved,
Where memory lingers most,
Or will it rest, as promised,
With the Lord and Holy Ghost?
One prays the spirit rests in peace,
But should mine not conform,
Please let it stay where beauty is
Near the place where I was born.

BERYL DYSON,
Gt. Livermere, Bury St. Edmunds.

TODAY AND TOMORROW

From dawn of time, to present day,
On fields of battle men have lay
Wounded and dying for our fair land,
Tormented souls, like grains of sand
Strewn far and wide, to God knows where.
What is it for? And is it fair
That men should die, little more than boys
With youthful thoughts and promised joys,
Eager to answer their country's call
Though many are maimed and many fall,
Screaming voices in barbed wire,
Moans of dying among the mire,
Machine-guns singing their death knell,
Canons roar in this man-made hell?
All is now quiet, peace reigns once more.
It's finished. For their sake, let an end be to war.
We remember them all, down thro' the years
For the life they gave us, thro' their bitter tears.
So sleep brave warriors, your job is done,
For your greatest battle is finally won.

WALTER HUTCHINSON,
Hemsby, Norfolk.

EVENTIDE

The sun sinks down beyond the trees,
The world begins to take its ease.
The daylight ebbs like an ocean tide,
The moon and stars, set the day aside.

The dusty shadows climb the wall,
The bats begin to squeal and call.
The birds sit quiet in the bush,
Like man enjoys the peace and hush.

The cattle lowing in the fields,
Sleep and digest their evening meals.
In a gentle breeze, the corn crops sway,
As the fading light, marks the passing day.

The traffic now is on the wain,
Now it's safe, to cross the lane.
The engines now, are winding down,
The drivers, to their homes are bound.

Let's wish goodnight, to one and all,
With a whispered, gentle call.
The darkness comes, we see no more,
We'll turn the latch, and close the door.

DONALD FUTER,
Bardney, Lincolnshire.

WITHOUT YOU

Two words that speak grey thoughts
of vacant numbness.
A future that is only made of past.
To go forward is unthinkable
and backwards is impossible.
My heart is searching for that
peaceful place at last.

I look around and see that
all continues
blind in the knowledge of today.
Take heed of all those precious
moments, and store them carefully
away.
The need for them will one day
be apparent, when all that's real
disappears.
I ask the question "why?" so often
whilst drowning in my unshed tears.
Your thoughts and fears are with
me always.
I hear your voice at every turn.
The love and joy in our existence.
That path, that many more would
yearn.

BERYL M. PEPPERELL,
Whitchurch, Cardiff.

CHANGING WINDS

She caresses me,
Slowly.
Deliciously.
Her warm breath
Insistent.

Her ethereal arms
urge me down to lie.
Oh, she teases!
She plays.

She lulls me
into false lullabies.
With swiftness
of surprise
she twists and turns.

Her jagged edge
tears my heart.
She blinds me.

With vicious icy breath
She penetrates.
I take her full force
till limp, she leaves me.
Her scent - the only memory
She leaves ..

DIANE S. WILLIAMS,
Windermere, Cumbria.

MASQUERADE

Are you honest - tell me true
You answered "yes" - shame on you
An honest person answers "no"
Think a moment - you will know.

You never cheated - never lied?
Never feelings tried to hide?
The reasons why - I did not ask
Your honesty is just a mask.

The truth is stark - it burns the soul
It crucifies but makes you whole
Lies are cheap - they slip and slide
Their purpose is the truth to hide.

Truth is like a laser beam
Searching out your inner dream
Shining on each darkened spot
Showing up the putrid rot.

The truth is pure, it's strong and light
Separating wrong from right
Honesty is just a key
Which leads to truth for you and me.

SONIA ELIZABETH RICHARDS,
Exeter, Devon.

SUMMER

The heat moulds itself to the body,
An airless fit
Without breathing space,
Clamped on.
Although the body rears up to shake it off,
It will not be broken.
There, the honey warmth and spicy smell of skin,
As tears of heat channel down folds and enclosures
To meet in sequence, in a pool.
Noisome insects on cat-mint, herbs and honey-suckle,
And bees inside yellow poppies,
These deep scents together,
The summer incense settles.
Ants scale limbs and have a rude shaking down
But birds are hidden away.
Distant, the farmer works the hay in the rhythm of the years.
Uneasy motorists huff and hang out of windows
As they travel down the speed-less lanes
Then chase the cooler air of pace.
The day which does not move
But seems with us in perpetuity
Only changes its consciousness.
The eye strays to the glitter of the usual, made a celebrant
And granted some strange divinity
In this yearned for day.
Some sense of short splendour is in us,
As a later breeze moves us
To wandering work.

SUSAN W. WOOD,
Cartmel, Cumbria.

SPIRIT FRIENDS

We were once together you and I,
　　Sharing our love.
Then you had to leave and I was alone,
　　I was alone - Oh! No.
Spirit of light come near,
Nearer to me at this time.
Awake in me all heavenly beauty.
　　I hear music
So strange and sweet.
　　I see your face,
Sense your presence closer now.
Spirit friends gather with you.
　　Are you waiting for me?
I see colours - so soft,
Around you, Spirit friends.
　　The music is enchanting,
I will be with you soon.
Then I will dance
Before the Creator of all.

EDNA SAVAGE,
Southampton, Hants.

RESPONSIBILITY

How Can it Be -

When wraith-like mists curl o'er the hills;
When sunshine wakes the quiet of the Vale;
The bird-song carries on the breeze -

How Can it Be -

When frost-rimed tiles are first to light the eyes;
When smoke-grimed stacks tower high into the sky;
The pigeons strut across the cottage roof -

How Can it Be -

When realisation comes at dawn
That there's small future - only paths of pain:
The bed-side lamp - still lit - that cheered the night -

How Can it Be?

Oh, it can be -
Our days snatched as we may.
Some cry, some sigh, some whistle on their way.
The Lottery of Life can be unfair to some;
But all must share the awesome weight of blame.

No one being causes pain of war:
No one being takes the food away.
No one being shatters hope for peace -
Or fights to reach his Mecca, come what may.

The fairness of the hills,
The grimness of the ways,
The sadness of the sick,
All must be shared until that Easter Day.

FRANCES ALDER,
Kirkby-in-Cleveland, Middlesbrough.

REFLECTION

I walked a while and thought a while,
And as I walked I wore a smile,
And as I travelled o'er the sod,
I thought of nature and of God.
The hills and verdant pastures green,
Upon that inward eye were seen,
In all the glory that abounds,
From valleys to the highest mounds.

The river winding o'er its way,
With silken sheen and glistening spray,
The trees and the wondrous flowers,
The birds in the leafy bowers,
Colour of every tint and hue,
Reflected in the mountain dew.
Oh! Who can doubt the Lord on high,
When walking 'neath such magic sky.

ANDREW SMITH,
Worle, Weston-Super-Mare.

THE PEBBLE ON THE BEACH

I walked along an Eastern shore one lovely Summer's day
And came across an ancient stone tossed in from the bay.
It was brown with streaks of gold, black and white ones too,
It stood out from the others with its many splendoured hues.

How long had it been travelling there - ten thousand years or more?
Rubbed smooth by many oceans from some far distant shore.
Was it spawned in waters cold or was the heat its sire?
How many stories could it tell of ice, or snow, or fire.

Glistening in the water, so clean and shining bright
I couldn't overlook it, it was a sheer delight.
I plucked it from its sandy bed and took it home with me
And placed it on my window sill for everyone to see.

But what a disappointment in the sunny light of day,
My pretty little pebble was now dull and drab and grey.
Gone were the pretty colours that attracted it to me,
It was no longer lovely without its parent sea.

Should I return it then, for things you once possess
No longer seem so wonderful and lose attractiveness.
Without the encircling water it was colourless and plain.
The pebble changed as it dried out and was just a stone again.

PAULINE J. ANDERSON,
Cambridge.

MARKET DAY

Hustle, bustle, busy feet,
Sounds of movement in the street,
No time to lie abed and sleep,
Today is Market Day.

Car horns hooting, beep, beep, beep,
Carts a-clattering down the street,
Everybody going there,
To the market in the square.

Trader's with their wares displayed,
Carts with awnings all arrayed,
People looking for to buy,
At the stalls with goods piled high.

There's the Baker and the Butcher,
There's the fruit and veggy man,
Shout, today's the day for bargains,
Come and get them while you can.

The pens for the animals, are in
The middle of the square, and
Sheep and Pigs with startled eyes,
Look out and simply stare.

Yet everyone's without a care,
They love the market in the square,
It's such a lovely day today,
Hooray, hooray, it's Market Day.

JOYCE MAY,
Birmingham.

IMMORTAL MORTAL

Shed no tears today for me,
I am am not dead.
I am in the warmth of a summer day,
I am in the laughter of children' play.
Save your tears, do not cry,
For whilst you live I cannot die.
Seek me in a star-strewn night,
Seek me in a swan's graceful flight,
Seek me in a spring's falling rain,
Seek me in a flower'd lane.
Where you seek me, there will I be,
For rests in you my immortality.

BERT LEONARD,
Rhiwbina, Cardiff.

THE POET

The poet's voice is rarely heard,
His thoughts combined to pen and ink,
Those feelings transferred into words
Which makes the reader sit and think.

What visions lie within his mind
Like music flowing through the air,
Words when written, not always kind
But the poet writes without a care.

His world is one of words and dreams,
His life is one of man possessed,
Once read his work brings forth meaning,
Once read, you see him at his best.

DAVID RICHARDS,
Pontypridd, Mid Glamorgan.

LEICESTER, EARLY MORNING

The stray dog barked 'til he was hoarse
Just as the day was dawning;
The pigeons signalled "R" in Morse,
In Leicester, early morning.

The pushlights bleeped their warning note
Upon the Pelican Crossing,
Whilst milk-crates rode on whining float
A-jingling and jossing.

The pavement-sweeper plied his broom;
The shopman tugged his awning;
The newsboy whistled out of tune
That bright and sunny morning.

The city clock began to chime;
The sunbeams grazed the house-tops;
The gully-cleaner gulped its slime
While queues formed at the bus-stops.

The post-man trudged with heavy sack
Just as the day was dawning;
The shunter paced on distant track
In Leicester, early morning.

JOHN MICHAEL CHAPPELL,
Leicester.

A FLOWER IN THE WILDERNESS

A flower grows in the wilderness.
What type of flower shall it be?
It does not matter, for in our mind's eye,
it can be anything we want it to be.
A poppy, a rose, a pink carnation,
picked with such loving care,
and placed on the graves of loved ones there.
A flower chosen, with tender care,
for the brave soldiers who died in the war.

Sometimes the flower will bend from side to side
when the harsh winds blow. But it will still be
standing tall, when the harsh winds go.
The rain will pour down and the flower will
wilt, and bow its head as if in defeat;
but the rain will come, and the rain will go,
but the flower still stands tall and begins to grow.

A flower grows in the wilderness and soon many
more shall grow and the single flower stands
alone no more, as a blanket of flowers
begins to cover every inch of the floor;
and every colour of the rainbow there will be,
for it stands for every colour, of every flag,
of every country, for the brave soldiers who
fought in the war.

A flower I would give my father who fought
in the war - a single red rose - a token of my
everlasting love for him, that grows and grows.

WYN WILKINSON
Wednesbury.

WHO AM I?

Who am I? Who can tell
The depth of emotions,
Secrets of desire
Locked in a heart to dwell?

Who am I? Who can see
The motivations of actions,
The blunders and caring
Brought forward by decree?

Who am I? Who can know
The heartache, the sorrow,
The joy and good cheer,
The attempts for happiness to sow?

Who am I? Who can comprehend?
Is it pride, is it fear,
Arrogance or stubborness
That will not let him bend?

Who am I? Who will hear
A plea for affection,
A faint voice from within
For the one who's held so dear?

Who am I? Who can feel
Not with hands that touch,
Get close even inside,
For the personality all will reveal?

TONY STYLES,
Weston-Super-Mare.

TO THE MAYFLY

Dance your briefest hour away,
Soon 'twill be the close of day.
You have known so little sorrow
You shall know no glad tomorrow.
Little heeding, little reck,
An infinitismal speck;
Haste, oh haste, now come away,
Soon 'twill be the close of day.

Dancing in the noon-day sun
Soon your little life is done;
Such brief happiness, alas,
Make the most of what will pass.
No one grudge your hour of bliss;
You were born today for this.
There is no one can deny
All shall perish by and by.

Taste the nectar, sip the dew,
There are hours all too few.
Fly on iridescent wing,
Listen to the cricket sing.
Chasing shadows in the sun -
That will be your life's work done.
Life is one long holiday,
Work tomorrow, play today.

So, for man, too, life is short,
Death will have its little sport;
Better sleeping, better dead,
Armageddon looms ahead.

Life can never be so dull,
Seek to live it to the full.

ALBERT BUTTERWORTH,
Halewood, Liverpool.

SHADOWSCAPE

Bright shadows, crisp and clear from morning sun,
the lacework of a leafless winter tree
sharp etched on pristine snow, a replica
traced like an outline for embroidery.

Green shadows, dark and cool 'neath leafy oaks
and river banks where willows lean and drape
their trailing fronds, to hide the speckled trout
in darkened weeds that camouflage his shape.

Silver shadows cast by pale moonlight
so sofly merge into obscurity.
Shy mouse will venture forth and end his quest
in barn owl's claws, for his temerity.

Shadows deep as night's black velvet cape,
the hours when fancy and illusion reign,
each shadow the epitome of fear
till sunrise walks among them in disdain.

Purple shadowed thoughts encompass days
when sadness weaves its thread of destiny,
for the shadow that accompanies through life
one day must fade and find eternity.

FRANCES WINFIELD,
Fishtoft, Boston, Lincs.

THE THIEF OF JOY

Eyes that once sparkled with laughter
Stare unseeing, vacant and blue.
Legs that once raced over unprinted sand,
Walked for miles where wild berries grew,
Now barely able to stand,
Shuffle forward - then forget where to go.

Sometime between fifty and sixty
A joker scrambled my brain.
Came like a thief in stealth
To steal all my joy - my health.

Hands that protected without fear
All that I once held dear,
Now tremble and shake with the effort
Of holding a half-filled glass.

He stole my speech, my past and my future.
Erased faces, names, birthdays, memories.
Scattered independence and pride.
Sieved the essence from family life.

When this empty sham of a body
Finally sloughs back to dust,
Then the joke will be over at last.

And, if you keep alive the memory
Of how it used to be,
The laughter, the tears
Of so many shared years,
Before Alzheimer scrambled my brain,
Then the joke will be
On him.
Not me!

JANET CULLUP,
Cherry Hinton, Cambridge.

SOMEWHERE IN BETWEEN

'Twas after the rain; the April rains
But before the Autumn leaf;
'Twas somewhere in between.

'Twas after the snowdrops and the snow;
After the daffodil's golden glow
And the violet's purple sheen.
But before the red and yellow leaves:
Before the fiery Autumn trees;
'Twas somewhere in between.

Between two seasons wet and cold;
Between them both it did unfold; -
The perfect, perfect dream.

'Twas absolutely glorious,
A picture so harmonious.
The trees were dressed in green.
Corn unveiled its yellow gown,
Rape unveiled its golden crown.
'Twas such a pretty scene.

Hedgerows gleamed; completely decked
Showing flowers gently flecked
With fruit which lay between.
Brown rich soils of texture defined
A landscape of colour, and beauty-entwined;
'Twas 'Heaven' - in between.

'Twas after the rain; the April rains
But before the Autumn leaf;
'Twas somewhere in between.

HELEN DEBORAH BENNETT,
Cardiff, South Glamorgan.

DREAM

I wound down the opaque window of my mind,
Seeking the long ago, tomorrow and today.
I saw a desert-scape of arid sand,
Rippled by a long forgotten sea,
With scattered shells that were my memories,
Empty shells that once contained my dreams.
Now polished by the silent scouring sand,
But still I glimpse my hopes, my fantasies.
Was I another one of fortune's fools,
Who thought that these were mine to command?
One who daubed the future bright? But no!
I gripped the rail and set my fancies free.

JACK GODFREY,
Roath, Cardiff.

JANUARY SUNDAY

Hurtling along through the night in the fog;
everything's airbrushed, nothing is sharp.
Cars don't exist, just streams of light,
red rivers, white torrents, odd yellow drops.
Trucks, slabs of grey with their edges erased,
lumbering monsters with misty cream halos.
Hurrying north through the fog in the night,
adding exhaust to the veil round the lights.
Speeding along 'neath a circus tent ceiling
of orange and yellow and tall metal poles.
Piles of bridges like soft woolly girders
then silence and fields and hedges and home.

MICHELLE GIBSON,
Balsham, Cambridge.

SNOW STORM

Bitter gusts echoed down the hills,
To sob through the sheltered valleys
Bearing with them whirling snow-flakes,
Dancing white-clad maidens lifting
Skirts a 'twirl to clear the dusty earth,
Shedding snow jewels from their gowns
To form a glistening carpet 'neath
Twinkling feet now patterned there.
The last carnival of winter,
The country-side deceived by early buds.
Birds in eager flight from warmer climes
Raise lilting songs to add to the deceit ...
Stilled when Spring is seen as a false promise,
As snowy fingers stretch across the meadows.
Despair not, for yet, there is still hope,
Within the church-yard's gloomy walls
A small, white blossom struggles to the light.

DAVID L. JENNINGS,
Belper, Derbyshire.

POLLUTION

I walked the banks
The serried banks
Of rushes by the river.
And the sightless eyes
Never saw the flies
As they darted hither and thither,
Confident, or so it seemed.
The enemy who arched and gleamed
Lay torpid in the river.
Still and confined
Their beauty outlined
In snowy foaming bitter
By-products of greed.
The careless deed
Had killed the shining river.
Had sucked away the oxygen,
Slain the gleaming denizen,
And thus beneath the trees
The May fly played at ease.

LINDSEY J. LONGVILLE,
Llandaff, Cardiff.

THE ISLAND

A million years of moon ago and all was ice
and white.

Ten thousand years of moon past;
Gulf Stream and receding glaciers
reveal a thousand islands scattered in the north,
fashioned by storms from the occident.
And one - just one - is holy, with a presence there.

Moon and sun, a thousand years distant,
the same small island.
Cliffs on the west, flat on the east,
- roosts guarding the nether shores,
the saint and martyr praying amid the farmers and the stones.

A hundred years of moon ago,
the monastery's gone - and ruins dot the hill.
The cliffs receive the first petrel from Hirta.

Ten years ago - and those western cliffs, impassive,
gaze towards man's edifice on the deep.

Today - the oil came ashore
and covered the cliff-base under a full moon.

And all is black.

PAUL HEPPLESTON,
East Grinstead, West Sussex.

SUNRISE

How I love to see each morning,
The rising of the sun
At the start of almost every day,
Till that day is nearly done.
As I gaze across the meadows,
I can see with naked eye,
Then suddenly a crimson glow
Appears across the sky.
I watch it as it changes,
Its wonders to behold.
A wondrous creation,
As its splendours all unfold,
Then the crimson slowly changes
Into glorious rays of gold,
Spreading beams across the sky,
That bring beauty still untold.

It slowly keeps on rising,
Shining from a clear blue sky,
With now and then a whispy cloud
Just gently floating by.
This is one of Nature's beauties,
That I very rarely miss.
It gives a chance to look upon
A scene of utter bliss;
And as I stand there watching,
You may hear me say,
Thank God for the Sunrise,
As we start each brand-new day.

WILLIAM KITSON,
Westwood, Nottinghamshire.

POEMS

Thoughts within a tranquil, yet ever-searching
mind,
That contain untapped verse and rhyme.
Awaiting the moment to be unleashed,
Each creation, in its given time.
Leaving open the gateway,
For increasing knowledge, and creativity.
Producing written works of art,
That are there, for all eternity.

WILLIAM KITSON,
Westwood, Nottinghamshire.

THE GARDEN

I love the garden
Especially in spring
When the flowers are peeping through
And the song birds sing
When the air is fresh
With a gentle breeze
Whispering sweet nothings
To the swaying trees
Where the tulips break through
A portrait of colour
Under the clear blue sky
And the daffodils trumpet triumphantly
For the likes of you and I
So much pleasure in the garden
Looking at the flowers
So quiet and peaceful
I could stay here for hours.

JUNE L. JOHN,
Llanharan, Mid Glamorgan.

SARAH'S SONNET

I once compared you to a Winter rose,
Which shines with beauty in the bitter cold,
You cut it, saying, "It shall beauty lose.
'will wither, die and fading not grow old".
The rose cut off from nature slowly died.
Yet, a young bud upon the stem lived on,
Clinging to life like hope in tearful eyes.
I said, "It lives and never shall be gone".
Outside, I planted it and it still lives.
I care for it to make it bloom in Spring,
To it warm kisses and sweet words I give,
To feed some hope and ease the pain within.
I do not save it that it live for me,
But so it live uncut, unhurt and free.

RICHARD L. WISEMAN,
Hythe, Kent.

RAPE FIELDS AT TRANBY RISE

Gold-shimmering in brilliant summer light,
The mass of rape flowers spread across the Weald;
Harsh vivid yellow, stinging sharp, so bright
The trees stood black against the molten field.
The perfume drifted in the heavy haze
Like pungent incense, peppery, thick and sweet,
Whilst dusty bees, attracted by the blaze,
Grew drunk and lazy with this golden treat.
I plunged deep in amongst the blooms, chin-high,
Drowning and floating in this sea of flame;
Powdered with pollen, choking, nostrils dry -
Soon glad to stumble back to whence I came.
Panting, I gazed, half-blinded by the fire,
And felt like Midas in an English shire.

MAUREEN CRONIN SETTLE,
Scunthorpe, Lincolnshire.

MEMORIES - DEMOLISHED BIRTHPLACE

In callous earth -
With broken bricks in disarray,
Tall willow-herbs of vivid flare
Reflect the dawn of day.

And gazing here -
The bride and groom with future schemes,
Fulfilled their hopes, desires, and plans.
In laughing joy, in many dreams.

And on this spot -
In protest calls at unknown hurled,
New babes called out their pristine cries,
In welcome, home and world - as I.

And standing there -
Two brothers glared with make-shift spears,
More personality than wrath,
With smiles, pretended fears,

Here branches spread -
From hopeful pip the mother set,
Her tree, with apples hard and rare,
Crab-taste, sweet to the zest.

Here Death clutched swift -
And finally hushed the agonized calls,
The fears, the questing eyes of child;
And laughter died within these walls.

One backward glance -
Tall willow-herbs inflame the site,
Symbolic pyre to desolate spot;
The seeds fly past, as family's flight.

Echoes ... Echoes ... The wind ... The memories.

FRED ALSTON,
Bury, Lancashire.

THE MAY TREE

Young and tender the may tree grew
Being planted with care by one who knew
How to make a garden glow
In Edgbaston so long ago.
Slowly over the passing years
It grew and blossomed to shed red tears
As spring to summer hotly turned.
Orange red the berries burned
Beneath the dark green brittle leaves.
Blackbirds, starlings, came as thieves
To gorge upon the pithy hoard
Till only leaves yellow autumn stored.
These dropped around the rough barked bole
Where myriad roots their nurture stole
When winter rains and icy storms
Had broken down their shapely forms.
Then nature's cycle once more turned,
Again the leaves and berries burned -
This time with destructive fire:
On Guy Fawkes night 'twas made a pyre.

JEAN LOUIE BLUCK,
West Heath, Birmingham.

THE RED ROSE AND THE LADY

A red rose whence first meeting you,
And now another at the end.
In good times you were my lover,
And now, just a far-off friend.

The red rose sends you all my love,
And my feelings as we depart,
The colour of the red rose
Describes my bleeding heart.

Remember me, my darling,
Do not let our memories die.
You will always be my Lady,
The red rose tells you why.

Without you life is empty,
Nothing seems worthwhile.
But thoughts of times I spent with you
Can sometimes raise a smile.

We met, we loved, we travelled,
And now we are apart,
And when you see a red rose,
You will know you're in my heart.

ALWAYS.

PAUL DAVIS,
Buntingford, Herts.

A PASSIONATE YUPPY TO HIS LOVE

With Apologies to Marlowe

Take my hand and dwell with me, and all delights will come to thee
Of tors and dells and verdant leas, and Alpine heights and sparkling seas.
We shall fly to sunnier climes and every morn be up betimes,
To swim and drink beside the pool, and, in the evening, play the fool!

Our home shall be a penthouse fair, you, the Queen that ruleth there.
Your every wish shall be my task, love in return is all I ask.
Your clothes shall be designer made, their vibrant colours ne'er shall fade.
Your shoes of kid, all furry lined and silver stars all intertwined.

A sash of satin, a stole of fur, diamond rings, perfume of myrrh,
All of this is thine to see - take my hand and dwell with me!
Servants you'll have to cook your meals, Chauffeurs to drive your life on
wheels,
TV's and Videos, computers too - all of this for me and you.

We will surf the Internet, our mobile 'phones the latest yet.

If this is how you yearn to be - Take my hand and dwell with me!

JOYCE MARGARET JONES,
Cambridge.

CLOUD THOUGHTS

So strange the thoughts that fly around
the inside of my mind,
like clouds across the sky, they're found
moved by a restless wind.
"Where do they come from?", ask you may,
"or where, indeed, they go?";
as clouds direct the weather's play,
they motivate me so.

Oft times my thoughts were pure and white,
in a gentle stream they flew;
fleecy clouds of cottonwool bright
against the deepest blue.
At other times, dark is my mood
with greyness all about;
stormy skies do the sun occlude
and put the light to rout.

And at such black times I may get
a thought as clear as light,
like forks of lighning in the wet
that shine startlingly white.
Like high charged clouds my thoughts are blown
all uncontrolled and free,
but, unlike clouds no-one can own,
they all belong to me!

GEOFFREY LUNT,
Worle, Weston-Super-Mare.

PONDERING

In thoughtful mood I sit with pen
    Reposing in my hand
And ponder on the things I see
    But fail to understand.
The conflicts all around the world,
    Hearts broken far and wide,
Victims of the onslaught
    Who're caught up in the tide.
So many shed their blood and tears
    As they rally to the call,
I ask myself, "Does this make sense?"
    And answer, "Not at all".
We build our ivory towers
    And castles in the air,
We try creating friendship
    With people everywhere.
Someone comes and plants a bomb
    And now there's nothing there.
This surely wasn't meant to be
    A part of nature's plan.
There must be at least a spark of love
    Left for our fellow man,
The world can not be perfect
    Until men can agree
In thoughtful mood to sit with pen
    And ponder just like me.

DAVID LIVINGSTONE,
Kirkby Lonsdale, Cumbria.

ASSISTED PASSAGE

My life is a lonely ocean,
My body is my raft,
Virtually I am oarless
Like every other craft.

I must have a destination,
Or drift without an aim;
I must employ my energy,
But never look for fame.

I must keep myself in order
And think with clarity,
On thoughts and deeds of bygone times,
Of faith, of hope, and charity.

These elements of love and care,
Still help when I request
Whole love's assistance in my prayer,
To aid me in my quest.

BERT GARRADLEY,
Kitts Green, Birmingham.

DRIFTWOOD

This unassuming stick, this dried bleached wand
At some time was a supple branch,
Waving in gales, with glossy leaves.
Now bone-dry, bone-warm, bone-curved,
It lies beached, the wish of sea fulfilled.

The twist is smoothed, yet runnels lie
Gouged out along its length,
As if the sea's caress was loving once,
Then changed to fickleness.

Now old, deserted, cracked and weak,
The richness of its outer skin long gone,
It rests on salty sand, near salty waves
And takes on camouflage of snake.

The tide goes roaring on,
The sea tides come and go.
Nothing can reach the wood
To bring it back to life.

Ten hundred years from now
People will gaze and gaze;
This was a part of oak or ash
Held in a spotlight's glare.

What is a tree?

MARJORIE T. BROWN,
Exeter, Devon.

SOME THINGS WILL FADE

Some things will fade with time
only briefly flitting through my memory fine.
A summer's day, a winter's night
when love was new and all was right.
The heavenly stars twinkling above
that orange harvest moon, remember love
how honeysuckle spices filled the air
while blackberry thorns pricked your lady fair?
Cold nights of passion in your car
when blood ran hot though cramped we were,
we only feared the swiftly passing hour
that parted us, not man or shower.
Remember seeing pictures in the clouds
like children we saw them laughing aloud,
then when you had to go away
I waited so long and prayed you would stay?
You though, had another love, day and night,
stronger than I that bound you tight.
'twas music tearing always at your heart,
waking and sleeping, so we must part.
I see that piano standing there
older than I, not grey like your hair.
Will it love and hold you, give kisses so warm
as you turn in your sleep now I am gone?
You cannot say you don't remember me
as I will you throughout eternity,
for even though some things fade with time,
I once was yours, and you were mine.

ELIZABETH COWLEY GUSCOTT,
Fishponds, Bristol.

ICE-MAN

The ice melts to reveal your long forgotten form,
Images of your near-naked ancient body
Clinging to the frozen rocks of the mountainside
Will haunt me forever.

You were torn from your homeland,
Exposed for all the world to see.
You lay there, your dignity in tatters,
Every inch of you invaded by unwelcome hands.

You must have been such a strong man in life,
How alone you must feel, how powerless against their prying eyes;
My heart bleeds for you,
Be strong, be still, you are not forgotten.

I never knew you in life, and yet I feel at one with you,
The Desire for life has stirred in me once again,
Give me the warm sun on my face,
Let me embrace once more the hillside's fragrant grasses;
Life is for living! I silently scream.

Wrenched from your 5000 year sleep, you radiate power and
Energy that astounds me,
How can one so long dead, awaken such emotions in the living?
I am no longer afraid of my own mortality, and marvel at the life
Force that still flows from your now fragile frame.

The memory of your face will never leave me,
So ancient, and yet so vibrant;
I will hold you in my heart until my own journey's end,
And will carry with me, your memory,
To rest in peace once more.

HELEN JONES,
Llantwit Major, S. Glamorgan.

OUR DERBYSHIRE VILLAGE

This is my home, cosy, and small.
I often stand at the old stone wall.
I gaze across the fields and hills
Towards the village of New Mills.
How wonderful it is for me
To find a place I love to be.
So many things to see and do,
Each hill you climb, a splendid view.
Quaint little pubs to call for a drink,
To sit and chat, or simply think.
Tranquil, quiet, calm and still.
I love our village, I always will.

IRENE COSTELLO,
New Mills, Derbyshire.

WHERE AND WHY?

The wood has vanished. Where has it gone?
The pines that fretted the full moon's face
Have gone. Uprooted stumps litter the churned up soil.
The brown owl and wood pigeon are no more.
The billow-sounding winds that agitate the branches
Are no more, the branches are no more.
The sunset flames no longer through them
But dips 'neath sterile horizon
And uninterrupted afterglow
Unbroken on forever.
The silhouettes of alder, aspen, birch
No more embroidery lay on the sky.
And to infinity, between slate cirrus clouds
And hazy distance on the ground, a nothingness,
A void - is left to ponder ...

DERRICK MITCHELL,
Southwell, Nottingham.

FROZEN IN TIME -

THE MINERS BRIDGE WATERFALL, CONISTON

Frozen hard in day's dark time
Coniston Fells persisting Force
Hand carved in triplicated stones
Weightier than deadened lead
A blackened line to define the source.
A form in bleak late winter's
Memory of sudden freezing March
With silent potent course
Of Church Beck's tumultuous flow
Gleaming under crystal daggers long
Festooned from darkened rocky cliffs
Edging brittle plates of tumbled ice
In alabaster's translucent glow.
Bedrocks glint in mica stone
And polyphanted organic shapes
Dark to light in varied tone
The miners' bridge above and adit
In western deep cut cleft
With sullen stones and mineral drapes
Of warmth and life bereft.
Summer brings a cooling breeze
From sparkling rushing waters
Shadowed by overhanging shielding trees
With cascade of fluttered variegated leaves.

Dr. DAVID CHARLES PEARSON,
Grange-over-Sands, Cumbria.

THAT MOMENT

If I had spoken at that moment,
Told you what I thought you knew,
Touched your sleeve as you were leaving,
Shown you how my heart was grieving,
Would you still have left me there
To live in regret and despair;
Or could that instant - thrown away -
Have begun eternity with you.

BERYL M. LAITHWAITE,
Southampton, Hants.

TO SPRING - A CONFUSION OF THOUGHT

Beloved herald - dare I claim you?
Dare I name you yet the solace of my lonely heart?
Incessant dreamer - must I doubt you?
Know about you, yet keep silent in a world apart?
Unknown intruder -
Usurper of the heart's solicitude,
Love's creator -
Late offspring of the soul's ingratitude,
Elusive phantom - strangely haunting,
Cruelly taunting, yet the prologue to my heart's rebirth,
I must receive her, though tormented,
My resented fate inevitable to the earth.

Intangible mist that hides the future from my eyes,
Veiled predictor, grasping fate between your hands,
Be kind. Do not destroy the faith I placed in you.
Be wise - or I may never see the distant view.

MURIEL McNEILL,
Birkby, Huddersfield.

ON HUMBER BRIDGE 5.00am

Standing here bathed
In the first light's haze
On Humber Bridge at 5.00am.
Tranquillity's translucent diadem
Dissipates the sadness
Along with the mist,
Which touches my mind
Struggling to come to terms
With its own most beautiful time.
I watch through quiet tears
As the moon surrenders
To the first amorphous kiss of dawn.
The soft grey does not blind
Like the hard white of day,
Or shroud as the dark
Instead achieves a perfect balance
Of the neutrality needed
By an unbalanced heart.
A tiny sailboat gently moves,
Caught up in my iris with my image of you.
A memory of change
Without sorrow
Waving goodbye as it follows the tide.
And if and when I choose to die
It will be morning.
For morning is a beginning
Never an end.
And it will be on Humber Bridge
At precisely 5.00am.

ALENE KIMM,
Mansfield, Notts.

THE SEEDS OF THOUGHT

You may laugh and wonder
At my love of Wallflowers dear.
The last flowers that my father gave me,
So profuse in seeds each year;
And, they are gathered carefully,
To plant again once more,
And, when they flower just the same,
Memories flood in so clear,
Of such good times in days of yore
Thoughtful, clearly in mind do stay.
Then, as each bloom once more appears
Thoughts will not fade away.
Their glorious scent and colours,
Reds, yellows, purple and mauve.
Oh! What a lovely gift it was.
An everlasting treasure trove.

PEARL MANSELL,
Exeter, Devon.

A COUNTRY WARDEN

Every day, I wake up to see
One more leaf upon the tree.
Another day, another dawn,
The countryside in early morn.
There's no-one else, but me about,
To stand and watch each leaf come out.

Thranslucent clouds cast ribbons of light,
Turn fields and hills to golden bright,
Weightless as cotton, on the breeze.
The warm wind whispers through the trees.
Nothing gives me greater pleasure,
Than to walk the countryside I treasure.

IRENE COSTELLO,
New Mills, Derbyshire.

JUST YOU AND ME

If I do not often speak your name,
   Do not think I do not grieve.
The words that come, so easily to some,
   Were never yours or mine.

Do not think you are forgotten,
   Because I do not make a fuss
In outward show, that for some others
               means so much,
   But never could be right for us.
As we were in life, so let it be,
   What remains unsaid, is what we were,
Just you and me.

JEAN L. ROUND,
Shard End, Birmingham.

AUTUMN LEAVES

A drift of gold in silvered mist,
A thousand memories,
Briefly fluttering to rest,
And melting in the fall.

Early memories of Spring,
Pearly dawns alive with song,
The quickening pulse, the flowing sap,
The future full of promise.

Soon, the threshold left behind,
Fulfilment floods the earth,
Lazy days of summer warmth,
When time itself stands still.

Or so it seemed, yet suddenly
There's crispness in the air,
A lengthening of shadows,
And tang of fading flowers.

But glory gilds the woodland scene,
Russet, copper, gold,
No fading in obscurity,
But glowing, blazing vigour.

Then nature, greedy for her own,
Recalls that fiery wealth,
The mists of dampness chill the sap,
The leaves drift down to earth.

A carpet now of memories,
Left when Autumn fades,
A treasure-house of golden dreams,
Perhaps, a tinge of sadness.

ELIZABETH STOKES,
Carlton, Nottingham.

NEWTOWN

The rain came down on the old new town
That even looked cold by day,
And when the light shone through
The grime shone too,
In another shade of grey.

They said the passing cars, the sun and stars
Were yours in the free for all,
But the heat of the sun
Had gone long before
You left those factory walls.

You seemed so slight against the stars
Without the price to pay,
While you missed the moon
When you worked those nights,
And slept the sun away.

Time was when the days were short,
You'd have held them in your hand,
Now you wish away
What once you felt
Was everything you had.

So quick the fright, that sudden chill
Which isn't from the night,
It's what you saw
And left behind
Attacking in your mind.

The rain comes down on that old new town,
It even looks cold by day,
And when the light shines through
You shiver too,
In another shade of grey.

MAGGIE YOUNG,
Cardiff.

ONCE UPON A WINTER

On panes, finger-drawn patterns in child's breath,
Had frozen overnight.
To become, by dawn, window scultures.
Sparkling iced engravings,
Against a background fresh-fallen and white.

Outside, flakes had formed cushions on benches,
Matching a carpet, beyond.
That had quickly spread over the hedges,
Across the herbaceous border,
And into, and out of, the pond.

Under the privet, tiny stars danced,
The lingering heads of borage.
And as traffic snailed by on un-roads,
We gingerly ventured forth, wrapped warmly,
And filled to the brim with porridge.

Beeches and oaks on distant hills,
Their foliage, long shed,
Resembled giants. Naked. With arms
Thrust up into heaven,
To grasp seagulls that wheeled overhead.

Gales that swept down the valleys then,
Cutting like knives, all the day,
Were as cold, and as cruel,
As a witch's heart
And made summer seem light-years away.

But out on the moor, drifts of heather
Ran crimson as blood in the snow,
While the forest had snowdrops,
The heralds of spring,
Just beginning to show.

MICHAEL PETER GOULD,
Carlton, Nottingham.

LOVE'S GHOST

There's a ghost that is with me wherever I wander,
From morning to evening, twilight till dawn.
It deepens my loneliness, fetters my freedom,
Sobers my happiness, laughs me to scorn.

Why must it haunt me, and walk in my footsteps,
Shatter my solitude, dance in my dreams,
Lurk in my shadow, and sit at my elbow
When daylight is done and the firelight gleams?

It maddens and taunts me what e'er I accomplish,
Gnaws at my hopes and banishes smiles.
Yet in spite of its torture I love this vague spectre,
Long for its company, wait on its whiles.

This wondrous wraith of my solitude's making
Is fathered by hope and mothered by fear,
Born of a wish that is my dearest longing,
Yet I dare not to hope that it's coming is near.

Senseless intangible dream I must find you.
I'll hold you, caress those lips made to be kissed,
Embrace you and crush you and keep you for ever
If ever I learn that you really exist.

PETER K. GREAVES,
Keyworth, Nottingham.

TO A STONE CIRCLE

The two jade eyes pronounced their doom,
smouldering an instant, and were gone.

It was enough. The wily Greek
had gripped the prickling nettles
of those writhing serpent locks -
and he held aloft the ghastly Gorgon's head.

The paralysing acid of those awful eyes bit deep.
The watchers stared in disbelief -
they stared eternally.
And in a trice - a lifetime on -
each sense seeped out, all feeling fled
from sinew, flesh and bone;
their bodies stiffened, blood congealed,
she turned each heart to stone:
each captive memory became
a dream beyond recall.
No mortal cure now could melt
the marble of their limbs,
no power unnumb their solid veins
or thaw the granite of her gaze -
the witch had cast her spell.

The magic of Medusa's glance
the centuries have proved:
the stones are standing where they stood,
unmoving and unmoved.

PETER WATSON,
Costessey, Norwich.

COW PARSLEY - IN PRAISE OF

On wings of song ne'er borne,
Or poet sing thy praise.
The country lane adorn
White filigree of lace.
Cow Parsley in abundance grow
Along the ribboned green.
Warm, pungent on the air prevails.

Slender arms raised up high
Starry eye'd, white flower crowned.
Proudly still, beneath a sunny sky.
Resplendid, in a bridal gown.
Queen Ann's lace, thy country name.
Graceful, in daintiness arrayed
Standing in the month of May.

Children play a tuneless note
Upon the hollowed reed.
Shrill and piercing, old ears do smote.
Countryways, timeless customs cleave.
Cow Parsley, the ruined mound enhances
And England's meadows green.
Familiar beauty blooms, unseen.

MINNIE WALTON,
Cotgrave, Nottingham.

THE LONGEST SLEEP OF ALL

When I die and life is over,
Lay my bones in fields of clover,
Be not sad that I am gone,
For my spirit in you lives on.

Do not weep upon my headstone,
Standing morbid all forlorn,
Caped in shrouds of deepest black,
Will not inspire the memories back.

Let the grasses blanket o'er me,
Pillowed on the softest earth,
In peace my bones will sleep below thee,
Fortified with gentle mirth.

Let beasts of field graze aside me,
With torrid birdsong overhead,
Grieve not that I am cold or lonely,
T'is not my spirit that is dead.

Do not please tidy this my tomb,
With floral sprays of neat cut bloom,
Let the rambling wild flower cover,
In chaotic beauty like no other.

Lament no more when I have passed,
For freedom will be mine at last,
Tears that fall in pain are shed,
Are tears in vain once I am dead.

Only one thing that I ask,
That two black horses draw my cask,
To lay me where the earth is deep,
To cradle me throughout my sleep.

PAULINE S. ROSE,
Catforth, Lancs.

SPRING SONG

All the world lies dormant, languid, waiting,
Beneath the great grey, cloud-filled, sunless sky,
Grebes, engrossed in their ritual mating
Dive, and are gone, in the blink of an eye.

Silver gleaming willow buds, now in bloom,
Green catkins, tossing on dark branches bare,
Black shadows, piercing through the thickets' gloom,
Contradistinctive in the cold March air.

Along the far side bank, across the lake,
Without a sound, a line of sheep file past,
Follow-my-leader is the path they take,
Stolid woolly faces, bent to the last.

The noisy magpie, silent now, flies down
To feast alone, on crumbs that I have thrown,
The gleaming feathers of her striking gown
Moved in disorder, where the wind has blown.

A misty calm and stillness steeps the air,
As only wild fowl from the distance, call
From far across the echoing waters there,
Forever seeking mates from rushes tall.

NORMA MOYLE,
Purley, Surrey.

THE TWILIGHT CAT

Why do you purr, my lady,
As you nestle upon my knee?
Is it because the evening breeze
Is whispering soft to thee?

Is it because the twilight
Tempts you to steal away,
To stalk its lengthening shadows
At the close of another day?

Or does the long grass rustle,
Inviting you to see
The myriad life that's stirring
In every silent tree?

Is it because the moon smiles
As she rides the sunless sky
Because she knows a secret,
Stars peep because they're shy?

Is it because the night time
Will hold for you no dread?
You'll share its strange enchantment
As I snuggle down in bed.

I know why you purr, my lady,
As you nestle upon my knee.
A little bit of magic
Is in that purr for me!

WIN SLATER,
Preston, Lancs.

THOUGHTS OF THE NIGHT

I love the dark evenings that engulf,
The cold winter days,
So bitter,
And damp,
So bereft of sunlight.

I love the world after nightfall,
When the wind rebounds,
From the Pilkington K,
Impenetrable,
Like the cover girl in Vogue.

When the howling turbulance from the North subsides,
I love the calm,
The quiescence of nocturnal peace,
Whispering in the shadows,
Agreeing to the conspiracy of silence.

I love the natural strobe of the moon,
Rocking gently,
Through an oak-lined silhouette,
Embracing the vast celestial canopy,
Under which I sit on my shaded veranda.

In the darkened streets so ambulent,
I love the echo of my lonesome step,
Pricking the ears,
Of insomnia,
The incipience of creative thought.

And in the hours of blind conception,
Aloft in the wind of somnolence,
In darkened harmony,
With nature and the mind,
I love the cohesion of the night.

ROGER BRINT,
Exminster, Devon.

TREES

Soft veils of spring and summertime,
Which hung in grandeur as a bridle gown;
Sparkling like jewels in red and green,
Adorning every limb of oak or ash;
So now in decay, they change to gold or brown,
Their earthly time drawing to a close,
Released - to gently fall.
Swirling, drifting on the breeze,
Silently touching Mother Earth below;
Vanish, - trodden underfoot,
Gone, - forgotten as a dream,
As though they had never been born.
Bodies now in nakedness revealed,
In rugged beauty there for all to see;
The strength of heart, - humility.
'Til in due time, reclothed
With garments new and fair,
Stand elegant and proud once more,
To bow and curtsy in the storm;
Or as a parosol, that offers shade
From the midday sun, swift shelter
In the rain.
"Why change your cloak?
Why take away your outward beauty?
Why leave you thus bereft?
We question not or even understand!
While others in an emerald sash of fir
Stand ever graceful, calm, yet so forlorn,
To wear a robe that will suffice
Until eternity!"

JOHN ROLPH,
Shirrell Heath, Southampton.

THE HUSBAND'S DREAM

When I have finished work
At the end of a busy day,
I would like my wife to greet me
In a gentle loving way.

She would put her arms around me
And, standing on her toes
Will kiss me very softly,
In the way a sweetheart knows.

I'd change my working outfit,
Some casual clothes I'd wear
Then, when feeling quite relaxed,
Would join my Lady fair.

She will lead me to the lounge,
To my favourite fireside chair,
And sitting on my bended knee,
Would gently stroke my hair.

We would talk about the weather
And other family things,
As she helps me don my slippers,
Until the kettle sings.

I would light my old briar pipe
As she makes a pot of tea,
Then once again we'd settle down,
Just my Wife, my Pipe, and Me.

REG CURWEN,
Ratley, Oxfordshire.

BEAUTY - OR THE BEAST?

Who shall tame - the wild Atlantic ...?
Who shall stem its restless urge ...?
Who shall splash - with certain safety
Through its smashing, crashing surge ...?

Sparkling gems of kindred brilliance ...
Sapphire, turquoise - emerald, jade ...
Swirled kaleidoscope of beauty ...
Veiling treacherous masquerade ...!

See upon the restless surface
Shadows flung - from clouds on high ...
Now with blackened rocks uniting
Masking death - from passers-by ...

Oh, to walk - the glowing pathway ...
Rescue p'rhaps - the drowning sun ...
Blazing-red and ever beckoning
As once more - a day is done ...

Yet, we cannot leave the light-house ...
Lives depend on vigil, strict ...
Who dare leave a ship to founder ...?
Who can Neptune's thoughts predict ...?

Here, "imprisoned" - in our tower
Never would we seek escape ...
Never delegate such honour ...
Or from duty, abdicate ...

If "needs be" - Lord, quell the cauldron ...
Magnify our wondrous light ...
Save prospective wrecks - from Hades ...
Spare a "breaking heart" - tonight ...!

MURIEL JOYCE MALING,
Swaythling, Southampton.

THE SCHOOL OF FRIGHTENED PEOPLE

In this school of frightened people
Where the children have no mouths,
And the population passes by
In isolated crowds,

And the rich are always richer
And the poorest always poor,
And the stench of desperation
Issues from each cringing pore;

There's a sense of consternation
If you meet somebody's eye
And a hopeless kind of pity
If you ask somebody why.

There's a dark, unspoken secret
At the corner of each lip
And a tell-tale pen just waiting
By each trembling fingertip

And the shadowed frown that passes
Over every unlined brow
Is a terrified confessional
For what you're thinking, now:

But you'll only hear the footsteps
And you'll only see the feet
Of the thousand marching sufferers
Who terrorise the street.

It's the school of frightened people
Where the stink of fear prevails, -
Full of eyes that harbour secrets,
Full of lips that tell no tales.

SUSAN MACKLAM,
Radford, Nottingham.

BEYOND THE STARS

I know now that I have lived.
And if I never see another day as the last
Sunbeam splutters from its fiery womb.
And if the Earth retch and spew
'Til inside out and but empty shell.
And if the final rainbow unfurls and indigo
Is no more.
I care not.
For I have seen the meaning of life.
In her gaze, bewitched.
Our eyes as one.
And all life's joy is squeezed in but
A single tear.
Time is no more.
A moment is infinity.
I ride the sunbeam from her smile.
Her eyes, a million twinkling stars.
I am hungry, yet filled; out-singing birds,
Yet all is hushed; moved - yet unmoving.
I am glad to be a man.
And if we never meet again, I care not.
For one day she will join with me
As dust - whence we came; somewhere,
Out there, beyond the stars.
And life will be once more.
Her eyes will light a new world; her warmth,
The sun; her smile - a rainbow.

And I will care.

HARRY J. WEST,
Alvechurch, Worcs.

HEALER

For Dr. Mike Leonard

Not as a person
Loves a brother;
But more splendidly,
With an insight of you
As a person.
On you, I placed
The heavy burden of my trust:
Confidentiallity,
Mood swings,
Illogicallity,
My numerous illnesses,
Aches and problems.
On all occasions,
You eased
The misery of my pain:
With care,
Without irritability;
To the extent of your knowledge
And depths of compassion,
You healed me.
Thank you.

MAGGI SOLLI,
Weston-Super-Mare.

WHISPER

Whisper yes but not too loud
For in the walls the spirits crowd.
They come from many years gone by
To join with us - you and I
In the cavalcade of memories.

Share a passing glance, a look,
A letter and a picture book.
Recall a name, a time, a place,
Picture that once pleasant face.
Remember all the happy times,
All the lost unwritten lines,

A tear, a laugh, a cry in pain
But let it all be whispered,
In case it's born again!

WILLIAM E. DEMPSEY,
Solihull, Warwickshire.

SPRING

'Neath the hooded cloak of winter peeps this joyous child,
Smiles in gentle wonder and all the world's beguiled.
The barren earth lies sleeping, her riches held in store
And our eager hearts are waiting to welcome you once more.
Weary trees stretch out their limbs, sunbeams chase the rain,
Daffodils and crocus bloom and violets scent the lane.
The blackbird calls a greeting, the lark is on the wing,
For in all the season's changes, there's no fairer face
than Spring.

BARBARA DISTON,
Porthleven, Cornwall.

MOUNTAIN STREAM

Gliding serenely o'er sleek, rounded pebbles,
Gently caressing each low-bending leaf;
Tranquilly deep'ning to peaty-dark rock pools
Dappled by sunlight in changing relief.

Swollen by snow-melt to frothy cream torrent,
Angrily seeking a path that is clear;
Thrashing the branchlets it whips past in frenzy,
Hurtling on heedless in headlong career.

Dwindling to nothing and starved of its rain-source,
Trickling lethargic in high summer days;
Stony beds gradually yield secret treasures,
Quartz-lights reflected in Sol's burning rays.

Feathery ice-fronds creep out from the side banks,
Stilling the current then chilling the flow;
Cased in its coating of winter-white wonder,
It sleepily waits for its duvet of snow.

BRENDA DENNISON,
Stanwix, Carlisle.

POETRY FOR PEOPLE

Letters, sentences, just words upon a page,
Poetry for people, an ink-made stage;
Feelings on a platform,
Performing publicly,
Secrets better kept inside, perhaps, inside of me.

Bruises, cuts, self-inflicted wounds,
Bandaged by the words I write on rainy afternoons;
Scars to last a lifetime,
Surgery cannot heal,
Helpless to disguise the pain that poetry can feel.

Poetry for people, verses meant for lives,
Breathing, beating, lungs and hearts, where only love survives;
Letters, sentences,
Words upon a page,
Feelings freed through poems that my teardrops couldn't cage.

Dawn-inspired daydreams written in the dark;
Hope and fear-stained tears cried on benches down the park;
Secret paper records,
Diaries of me,
Confidential heartbreaks put on show for all to see.

Foolishness, sadness, a sign of something wrong:
That I can't tell another soul, but put down in a song:
The state of my existence,
The essence of me:
A lonely people's poet writing people's poetry.

ANDY JAMES,
Rhoose, S. Glamorgan.

WHEN

When pipes of Pan greet every dawn,
And man with childrens' hearts are born,
When man will give, not take,
And start a better world to make,
When children cry with joy, not pain,
And safely walk down shady lanes,
When doors on latch are left for folks to call,
And no graffitti spoils the walls,
When wars are history in the books,
And pollution no more destroys our brooks,
When love is the thing that conquers all,
And children grow strong, straight and tall,
When wheat on barren lands shall grow,
And sweet water throughout the world will flow,
When man can talk but not in fear,
And plan his life for the coming year,
When man can walk in other lands,
and be welcomed there with helping hands,
When man will talk of peace, not war,
And there's a welcome on every door,
When man as one will kneel and pray,
Then we will have reached the perfect day.

WILLIAM E. DEMPSEY,
Solihull, Warwickshire.

PLOUGHMAN

Each morning on my way to school
I'd see him
Solitary, stumbling over heavy clods
Behind the plough
Wheedling, warning with his cries
Of "Gee" and "Whoa"
The steaming, striving horses
On their way.

At dusk's onset when I came home
He'd be there
His bent and sagging outline black
Against the sky
Solitary, stumbling still
Behind the plough
And his voice still calling, calling
"Gee" and "Whoa".

IRIS M. SQUIRE,
Balsham, Cambridge.

THE SUMMER ROSE

The slender bud of summer rose
Nurtured by the rain
Opens up her petals to see the world again
The delicate scent and flushed pink bloom
Just like a velvet gown
Tempts the bees to visit her and sip her nectar down.
As summer days grow shorter
Her petals start to fall
But though she's gone her beauty
Is heartening to recall.

MARGARET MARTIN,
Ulverston, Cumbria.

CARDBOARD CITY

If they ask you why he died,
Tell them how he tried and tried -
And how he cried,
Until he grew old and cold
   And pushed the world aside.

If they ask you when he died,
Tell them it was long ago.
Tell them that you didn't know.
Tell them that it didn't show -
   'Twas all inside.

If they ask you where he died,
Tell them in a place he hated;
And only God knows who created
This thing in which he was
   Ill-fated to abide.

If they ask, where he went,
Tell them he was quite content
And indeed 'twas heaven-sent
   For him to rest.

Tell them that you saw his tears,
That he told you of his fears -
   Many times.

Tell them how you walked away,
How you passed him every day -
   And closed your ears.

MAGGI SOLLI,
Weston-Super-Mare.

A MULTITUDE OF SINS

And when she goes
I shall dig up the roses
and separate the hostas,
plant vegetables instead of annuals,
and set shrubs and perennials
in the place of flowers.

I will leave the camellias
and the azalea,
but I shall uproot the unproductive gooseberry,
and in its place
I will grow onions and leeks
and possibly potatoes - definitely tomatoes.

I shall not touch the Cox's Orange Pippin
that grew from seed - the core
carelessly thrown by my father
whilst he was trying to look at
a Reader's Digest Condensed book
that she cocked a snook at.

And he shall rest in peace in the garden
that will be mine.
And in it I shall grow
a Clematis and a Wisteria
and a fast-growing Russian Vine
that will bury, or at least hide,
a multitude of sins.

J. MARGARET SERVICE,
Dawlish, Devon.

BELOVED GRANDAUGHTER

As life stretches out before you
Be yourself, be strong.
You are you. Special and unique
With all your life to seek.
Your smile lights up your face
And gives you gentle grace.
These teenage years,
Will bring laughter and tears,
Joys and much happiness, so
Remember my dear,
As the years roll away
The seed that is sown
Is the crop which is grown.
Be loyal and true in all you do
While the breeze of life
Lays a carpet of leaves
For you.

PAMELA BARRETT,
Balsham, Cambridge.

REQUIEM

Remember me as I used to be
Not as you saw me last
Recall the days of happy times
Spent with me in the past

Instead of tears for what might have been
Smile for all that we have shared
A life so full of happiness
Made so, because you cared

And when you next see a rose in bloom
Or hear the blackbird's song
Remember me as I used to be
In the days when I was strong

For I would not wish for you to grieve
For the man I had become
Instead relive those memories
Of the days when I was young

So remember me as I used to be
Not as you saw me last
And keep me close in memory
In your present and in our past.

PATTI BETTS,
Glenfield, Leicester.

SEAGULL

Fly away across distant shores.
Fly upon the wing of heaven's love once more,
Take your chance and fan the clouds,
Watch the stars kiss the sun and cry out loud.
Fly away to dream, a magic to uphold,
Such precious secrets never to be told.
Escape the sorrow and the pain,
Never more a tear to shed again.
Breathe the air that feeds the tree,
Eat the seed that's falling free,
From its ties that wish to hold it fast,
Shake the sorrow that's not meant to last.
Fly beyond imagining.
Softest clouds, the gentle rain.
Past the sun, past the stars.
Cross over to the other shores.
Keep the memories gentle and sweet.
Bitter sweet,
'till next we meet.
Take the love that's offered now,
Make the moments last and how.
You can dance on each shooting star,
So spread your wings and travel far.
So fly away across distant shores,
Fly upon the wings of heaven's love once more.
Take your chance and fan the clouds.
Watch the stars kiss the sun and cry out loud ... I love you!

LYNNE HULME,
Bramhall, Stockport.

LOVE MUST NOT DIE

Lead me by the magic in your dear eyes
O'er dales and mounds and renes - which seem to be
Valleys and mountains, rivers, cloudless skies -
Enchanting, ever reaching out to me.
May all these dreams which lift my slumbered night
Until grey dawn returns my deep despair
Someday convert this darkness into light.
Tomorrow will your love again be there?
Ne'er shall regrets enter into my theme.
Oft, times together, precious and aware,
Transcending all life's passing problems seem
Devoted to one only central care
In which we two, in hope and loving can
Enrich our lives, my darling Sandra Anne.

A. D.,
Rumney, Cardiff.

A CALMING BREEZE

Sometimes,
I can feel
The soft falls of autumn calling,
Upon the golden meadows of my mind,
When I remember,
Looking so deeply within
The mirrors of your eyes,
That held so fast the dying whispers
Of past summers in their warmth,
That these dark shades of winter now
Could but never form.
And sometimes,
I can still feel
Without the goodbyes,
Your honeyed breath beside me
In the long tossing curls of night,
Upon my empty pillow,
Just waiting for the spring again,
And that
Extra touch of dawn.

NORMAN ROYAL,
Fairwater, Cardiff.

CHANGING SCENES

Summer's dappled shadows roam
Through branches leafed with green
The earth below this sheltered bower
With coloured landscapes gleam.

The sun escapes between the limbs
Of mighty trees or small
To gild the ground below their heads
With hues that never pall.

Each pass of day reveals again
An ever-changing scene
The colours melt to form anew
Bright as they've ever been.

Some shadows linger, tinged with gold
Where branch and leaf hold back
The rays from sun that seeks to find
The ground where colours rack.

The yellow that becomes a gold
The blue that shines so bright
The tiny whites that from the depth
Reach for that welcome light.

Each tree or bush has much below
To gladden and delight
When daybreak comes they open wide
Form chasms for the light.

This wondrous world, this changing scene
Is there beneath our feet
A little time to stand and stare
Would show the art complete.

JEAN K. MALONEY,
Knowle, Bristol.

THE SONG OF THE WHALE

I once did hear the sad song of the Whale
And I can't get the tune out of my mind,
The haunting refrain echoes desolate
Like the ocean trapped in caverns by wind.

I once did hear the sad song of the Whale,
The melody of a mammal so free,
Roaming the oceans in search of the krill,
Sliding through the undulant, heaving sea.

I once did hear the sad song of the Whale,
But the echoes are diminished and rare,
For Man has devastated their numbers,
And soon we'll not hear their desolate air.

I once did hear the sad song of the Whale,
But my heart is heavy with loss and pain,
Where huge herds roamed, a solitary Whale
Seeks an answer to its haunting refrain.

GWENDOLINE J. DOUGLAS,
Hull, East Yorkshire.

FLOTSAM

Youthful urges throbbing in reckless currents.
Sensual whirlpools of encounter.
I savoured the ebb and flow of passion,
floating on another tide, another sea.

Drifting, always drifting,
avoiding the entrapment of a union.
I would not cleave to pillars of strength,
nor seek a resting place for spawning.

The solid spars which others clung to
offered only shallow futures.
I slipped through the waters of convention,
spinning, whirling to another place.

Friendships formed and nurtured,
hoping to brighten dull pools of humanity.
Greed-driven vessels surging with vain contempt
did not touch the elusive flotsam.

I felt the undertow of vanity
down to proud and shining structures.
Yet knowledge and beliefs unweighted me
as I ascended through the tarry timbers.

Now my form is slower, smoother,
fashioned stronger by life's ocean.
I wait next to a gentle rock, floating,
still restless, but forever free.

MARY NELSON,
Millom, Cumbria.

MEMORIES FROM CHILDHOOD

Of all the many things I loved in childhood's far-off days,
The beech tree, just outside the garden fence,
That trailed her lowest branches down to brush the garden soil,
With all my heart I loved the best of all.

At every chance I'd slip outside and through the creaking gate,
Then, footfall hushed on years of fallen leaves,
I would walk along familiar paths within the fragrant wood,
Content to dream and wander all alone.

Unheeded, time would slip away while I still lingered on,
Entranced by scenes that changed from day to day.
The first pale violets nestling in their damp green cushioned bed,
A shining slow-worm basking in the sun.

Then wandering homeward once again I'd reach my favourite tree,
And standing, small, beside the massive trunk,
Gaze upward through the branches reaching out into the sky
Until they seemed to spin above my head.

In the evening, from my bedroom I would watch the moving boughs,
And hear the secret whispering of the leaves,
Inviting me to close my eyes and lay my tired head down,
Forget the day and welcome sleep again.

You will not find that quiet wood, that giant beech today,
Nor in an afternoon of sudden showers
Gaze spellbound as the re-emerging sun on branches, winter bare,
Transforms the shivering raindrops into sparkling gems.

On the gentle slope where trees once grew, delighting my young heart,
The traffic thunders down in endless stream.
But sometimes in the strange delusions of the night
I wander through the wood again within a dream.

SUSAN P. BLAKE,
Southampton.

NEW DAY!

As I awake in the early morning
To the thrilling sounds of a new day dawning,
I listen to the melodious call,
Of a wonderful greeting to one and all.

The blackbird, robin and the thrush,
Burst forth in song from every bush
Until the silence is filled with sound
From the throats of all, the notes abound.

The lark sings from wings on high,
Flying higher and higher in the sky.
Could we but hold those notes that thrill,
Of a dawn chorus that will soon be still.

The day creeps slowly onward,
The melodies linger on,
But the hands of the clock move forward
And all at once it's gone.

DOREEN FOX,
Croft, Leicester.

ENVY

Oh, how I envy him,
Suave in his white tuxedo,
Seated at the grand piano,
In the foyer of a West End store,
Gently tickling the ivories,
And knowing every score,
Playing the golden oldies,
Just to please the ladies.

This gig to him is just a drag,
For jazz is his real bag,
Jammin' where the lights are dim,
And the sounds within
Are progressive, new and blue,
And the cats blow till dawn.

But then perhaps he envies me,
For he can see,
From my bespoke suit and shoes,
That life is so easy,
And whilst he plays his dues,
I can spend like a peer.

THOMAS CANHAM,
Saltdean, Brighton.

THE RIVER COMPOSERS

Brewed from a witches' cauldron the Viper ran,
Oozed black, dipped in an ink well underground,
Pleats her skirt along the ledge,
Bull rushes stoop to soothe her brow,
Whilst two perch ruffle her silted bed.

The skin taut as parchment paper,
Viscous primed for the water skater.
He scribes upon her back a verse,
Then transfers the pen for a more skilful glance,
To the literal joust of a kingfisher lance.

Hovering, grammatically he checks the text,
Preened and adjusts his nibs.
Poised, dives with prowess,
Then accurately and precise,
Punctuates, by putting commas and full stops in place.

A Frog crouched upon his Lily-pad,
Translates the words into an Oratorical Repertoire
Under a maternal Autumn moon.
A Water Vole underlines the composites.
Finally, a Tawny Owl correlates and edits.

In a tizzy, whirls a River Boatman,
Blotching the comprehension by sticking his oar in.
The Owl took a break and ate the Vole for dinner,
With eyes bulged he reeled his tongue in ...
The frog had grown partial to the River Boatman.

Around a bend, tins gashed like crimping sheers.
Washing machines and the arteries of sewers.
A desert where nothing grows, she'll only now be seen dead in.
Torn and soiled, a dress once fit for the ball ...
Returns to the cauldron ...

KEVIN BRYANT,
Braishfield, Hants.

LIKES

Chocolate and cheese,
Standing in breeze,
Raspberry jelly,
A gigantic telly,
Seeing a movie,
Music that's groovy,
A cute little cat,
A big velvet hat,
These are the things I like the most
But I mustn't forget peanut butter on toast.

LOUISE DAVISON, aged 11.
New Costessey, Norwich.

HARVEST TIME

The juicy plums fall from the trees.
The scented flowers in the garden
attract striped yellow and black bees.
The shining corn sways up and down in the breeze,
like waves on the sea.
An engine rumbles, a dark shadow appears.
The harvester approaches,
its lashing teeth work themselves down the field.
The tractor brings straw down to the yard,
leaving a haze of dust as it goes.
Midges fly in the morning air,
biting children as they go.
The combine harvester goes home to sleep.
The farmer sets fire to the left-over stubble.
Smoke drifts across the countryside.
The fire dies down.
The black field waits for the next season.

SIMON ARMITSTEAD, aged 10.
Haxby, York.

DEAF

Never again can I have a conversation -
With my voice.
Never again can I enjoy the seas -
With my ears.
For I have lost my amplifier of sound
And my hearing has disappeared.

Never again can I enjoy laughter -
Like I used to do.
Never again can I feel the music -
That I used to listen to.
For I have lost my ability to hear
And I can't hear you.

Never again can life be simple -
As it may be for you.
Never again can I hear the kettle boil -
Like you do each day.
For I am deaf and I'm wishing
For hearing to come my way.

CLAIR WICKENS, aged 15.
Gosport, Hampshire.

THE MAGIC BOX

I will put in my box
a thunder storm
my football boots
a wasp's sting

I will put in my box
piles of blue
a hedgehog's spike
a dream of sonic

I will put in my box
the howl of a dog
the purr of a cat
a funny face

My box is made of
grey emeralds
a genie's wish
a flame from the sun
the biggest rain drop
a spider's leg
the mud from a giant's garden
the air tank from a space man

The lock and key are made of bamboo shoots
I shall have fun in my box.

JOSEPH NICHOLAS COLEMAN, aged 11.
Carlisle, Cumbria.

NIGELLA HISPANIA

Blue maiden from Spain,
With a faint exotic perfume,
Delicately sways
As she enters the room.

She wears a crown
Of magical shape,
With intricate carving
Of feathery make,
Enhancing with mystery
The beautiful face.

Tall and slender,
In a gown of blue
Of misty texture and hue.
Lending grace and charm
To her every move,
With love in her very mood.

Whispering enchantments
Like the gentle breeze,
Till parting comes.
Leaving a sense of wonder,
When one might say,
Here is captured the magic
Of floribunda
In every delicate way.

RONALD V. COOPER,
Brockley, Bury St. Edmunds,
Suffolk.

TO HAVE YOU NEAR

To have you near.
That such a tiny phrase could mean so much
That it should conjure up your very touch
And bring you near.

To have you near
Makes everything so very much worthwhile
Encouraged by the love that's in your eye,
Or p'haps a tear.

To have you near
Will come to me with ev'ry flower I touch.
I'll whisper that I need you, oh, so much
And want you here.

To have you near.
What sweeter symphony could ever be
Crescendoed from my heart to let you see,
I love you dear.

REGINALD B. JOHNS,
Sleaford, Lincolnshire.

MY SPECIAL RAINBOW

I walked feeling lonely, heart heavy with pain,
My tears went unoticed, they fell with the rain.
Head bowed, once more wondering, "Why me, why oh why?"
I glanced up for a moment, saw it there in the sky.

It stretched from the forest, right over the Park,
The beautiful rainbow, the colourful arc,
And then, for a moment, I thought it a sign,
Meant for my eyes only, I imagined it mine.

So awesome, so perfect, it stretched out above,
Like a banner of glory, a ribbon of love.
I seemed to walk through it, as I slowly strolled on,
And when I looked back, the rainbow was gone.

Just then I realised, it had taken my tears,
Had lifted my spirits, and help ease my fears.
Now calmer and stronger, I knew I would cope,
Then I quietly gave thanks, for God's symbol of hope.

I often think back, to that day in the past,
When sad and confused, I found peace at last.
And, I'll always remember, that day on the hill,
And the beautiful rainbow that strengthened my will ...

VALERIE ANN JONES,
Weston-Super-Mare.

A DREAM COME TRUE

My little boy will one day play
In a world with no tomorrow or yesterday.
I can hear his laughter, merry and shrill
In the only place where time stands still.

My little boy the horizon will run
Into a crimson setting sun,
Bounding like a rabbit, on the mountain crest,
I can see him now, his image impressed.

So many things for him to do,
So clear in my heart, it has to be true,
Just look at him, holding that bird in his palm,
May be I'll touch him, if I reach out my arm.

And then in the winter, what a wonderful pose,
As a snowdrop melts, on his little damp nose,
Talking to a snowman, on the brow of the hill,
With never a danger of catching a chill.

My little boy will awaken at dawn,
To the wonderful sight of a calf being born,
More precious to him than a much loved toy,
Are the things that will come to my little boy.

CYRIL JOHN LANGDON,
Brackla, Bridgend,
Mid-Glamorgan.

A POEM FOR SAMANTHA

Two long months to restore me,
But then Grandad could see,
The beauty within me.
I once was a tree!

The Tree

The shock of the axe cutting so deep,
I fell with my neighbours
As if fast asleep.
No more the rise of the sap in the spring.
No more the song birds my branches to cling.
Stripped of my mantle, naked we lay,
Leaves dying softly, to blend with the clay.

Long summers and winters pass unattended,
Until chisel and saw by the craftsman are wielded.
Can that be my skin, shining with light,
Moulded anew, contours aflame?

Born again am I. Loving hands to care.
Surrounded by laughter, and a family to share.
Samantha lies sleeping and smiling, I see,
Perhaps dreaming of a garden,
A swing
By the tree.

Restoration of the Bedroom unit carried out September 1987.
Unit fifty years old September 1988.
Poem and restoration by

RONALD KILEY,
Carlisle, Cumbria.

Grandad of Samantha.

MAKE IT LAST

To say it all and mean it is one thing,
To mean it and say it another.
To hold on fast to what you've got,
Given time again, discover.
Discover what life means,
With all its ups and downs,
Meeting people of the world,
From cricketers to clowns.

To unscrew and screw many times
The top of dreaded hate,
To hold one's tongue and take a chance,
To wait and wait and wait.
Feathered by nocturnal springs,
Groping in the past,
To find a sincere and worthy love,
To make it last and last.

MICHAEL K. LYNCH,
Chorley, Lancs.

EVENTIDE

I die
a little without her
at eventide
while sheep lay still on dark hills
and deer dance
as badgers burrow amid
the starlit carpet of leaves.
It is in the ghost-owl silent
shadow of night
that one falls apart
and the soul is mislaid
by the heart's greed.

RAY ANDERSON
Upper Shirley, Southampton.

GOODBYE HAPPY JEANETTE

I wish it were I who had married you that day,
I wish it were I who had had the vows to say,
I wish it were I whom the minister had blessed
And who had stood beside you in your pretty hat and dress.

I console myself, it was lovely to see,
You're happier with him than you would be with me.
As you walked with him hand-in-hand down the aisle
I saw such peace and contentment in your smile.
That look on your face I will not forget,
May your love grow stronger and stronger yet.
Goodbye happy Jeanette.

MALCOLM LISLE,
Gateshead, Tyne and Wear.

WHAT AM I?

Pinpricks of light in the darkness,
That is all we are.
Minute scraps of energy,
Each burning like a star.

Each with secret treasures
Mapped within the brain.
Where these ideas come from
No-one can explain.

Whether you're an Einstein
Or an ordinary Joe,
Do not let them label you
Peculiar or slow.

Do not let them label you
Single mum or *working class*,
Dyslexic or *disabled*,
Ignorant or *crass*.

You and I, we are unique
As every flake of snow.
Cares of life may disappear
But we reflect a glow.

Let's use the gifts God gave us
As we travel on life's way.
Use that inner spark of specialness
That never will decay.

MARY DAULTON,
Lincoln.

AS EACH DAY

As each day becomes history, memories are all that remain,
Happy thoughts and feelings, nobody else will explain.
Think of what the future holds, tomorrow's another fight,
Every second slips to the past; like turning out a light.

As each day slides to its end, welcome a grateful dead,
Just like thoughts and memories, nothing is ever said.
Even faded photographs, turn to dust in time,
Like bones in an ancient coffin, a toothless grin to shine.

As each day becomes the past, it's gone forevermore,
A fleeting glimpse of the present, we'll never know for sure.
Make mistakes and feel the pain; can't undo what's past,
Even the future's gone forever, nothing ever lasts.

As each day circles on, nothing will ease the pain,
Nothing, not even darkness, is there to take the blame.
With every advancing twilight, turning to forgotten years,
Memories are all that you have, happiness, sadness and tears.

PETER LAPHAM,
Lawrence Weston, Bristol.

CREATURE COMFORTS

It's beautiful here in the garden
As dusk falls all around.
The birds have gone to sleep to rest
But there's activity on the ground.

The scented smell of roses
Against the sky of red,
The hedgerows glisten like a thousand jewels
As the spider spins his web.

It's a wondrous night in the garden
On this tranquil summer eve,
The leaves are swaying overhead
From the whispering of the breeze.

It's never silent in the garden
With all creatures great and small
Nestling, foraging, wide awake.
God Bless them one and all.

SAMANTHA MALKIN,
Great Barr, Birmingham.

GOLDEN WEDDING ANNIVERSARY

For my Grandparents

From an ocean so blue,
To a corn field so gold,
A morning so fresh of glimmering dew,
Another glorious story of Love is told.

Many, years have passed, yet your honours maintain,
Sincerity still burns a golden flame.
Perpetual love, for what could prove this integrity,
Nothing, but a partnership of half a century.

DONNA HUBBARD, aged 14.
Waltham Chase, Southampton.

DREAMS

For Emma my daughter

Peaceful dreams of a sleeping child,
A silken web, weaving a hundred magic spells.
Dreams of sunshine holidays,
And the peal of Christmas bells.
Dreams of pretty butterflies, and angels,
Dressed in white.
Dreams of silken dresses, and a magic carpet ride.
A wonderland of fantasies, of jewels in the sky,
And dreams of cuddly animals, of woods where rabbits
Lie.
Sleep sweetly now my little one, for worries have
You none.
For all your dreams are happy ones,
A magic spell you've spun.

PAULINE ANN MURFET,
Beck Row, Suffolk.

IMMORTAL ROSE

Perpetual beauty, you must draw
Your colour from the morning star
Or from the glowing sky at eve
Wherever vibrant fires are.
Within your velvet petals' cup
Pearl tears from the cloud-strewn skies
I would your weeping beauty gleamed
Ever before our temporal eyes.
And when the night in shadows cast
To steal your radiance whilst we dream
I know in valleys far and vast
That you immortal rose are seen.

VALERIE AXE,
Wembworthy, Chulmleigh,
Devon.

DIMPSY TIME

That hour before dark, the dimpsy time
Is when I dream, an hour that is mine,
A cosy room and chair that's deep
To snuggle in, with slippered feet.
A feeling of warmth creeps over oneself,
I sink in a stupor and dream with stealth.
I try not to sleep, it's hard to resist.
Thoughts drift and float like Will-O-The-Wisp.
My head sinks lower and lower on chest,
A gentle snore, then a startled arrest.
This stupor where thoughts are dim and unreal
Is a respite from troubles, I try to conceal.
At the end of each day I fall in the trap,
In the dimpsy time, of taking a nap.

PATRICIA EVANS,
Exeter, Devon.

THOSE WERE THE DAYS

I still recall when I was small -
Against the house I bounced my ball,
And chanted, "rollsy, clapsy",
And, "round the world and backsy".
(Mother's patience sorely tried
As, "thud, thud, thud" was heard inside!)
Then came skipping in the playground,
Long rope turning round and round.
Children jumping all together,
Shouting rhymes about the weather,
Always counting up to twenty,
Making sure the rope was "empty".
And, if you ever fell at play,
You would surely rue the day;
The dreaded tincture was applied
(Do you remember how you cried?)
'Twas not the cut made you call out -
But iodine that made you shout!
Then came the war and every child,
Gas-mask in hand, to shelter filed.
And, underground, shared dingy lamp
With daddy-long-legs and the damp.
That dreadful siren spoiled our games
(We called old Hitler naughty names!)
At home, all curtains closed up tight,
Showing not a chink of light.
Air-raid wardens in the streets;
Food was rationed ... even sweets!
But folks were friendly and - what's more -
You *never* had to lock your door!

- *Those were the days* -

ANNE VERONICA BROWN,
Histon, Cambridge.

EXPRESSIONS OF REALITY

Looking through my glasses
I stare and gaze and look,
I scrutinise the sentences
On the pages of my book.

Looking through my glasses
I read about a child
With laughing eyes and smiling face,
She seems so meek and mild.

My eyes view all the good things
As well as all the bad.
The faces of the joyous ones,
The faces of the sad.

The men who always snooze on seats
With newspapers for sheets.
The families with their little ones
That stroll along the street.

The beauty all around us
In the freshness of the fields.
In the golden glistening of the corn
And all that harvest yields.

The seasons turning slowly round
From Winter to the Spring.
The auburn shades of Autumn
And the brightness Summer brings.

But looking through my glasses
I give the world a look
And decide that it's much better
Than the pages of my book.

WENDY CUMNER,
Eastleigh, Hants.

BLUE BEAR - TRUE BEAR

A collage of dreams.
A collage of schemes.
The picture eludes me
But I can see you
Quite clearly.

You stood in the corner
Lost and forlorn,
People looked and you
Were treated with scorn,
Surrounded by paintings,
Old carpets, bundles of newspapers
And boxes piled high.
No one really saw you
Except I.

Your fur was dingy.
Your ears in tatters,
But none of that
Matters now you
Have come home.

BEVERLEY BECK,
Binstead, Isle of Wight.

PICTURES

When I close my eyes
The pictures I see are
Visions and images of thee!

They flash through my mind,
They find me unkind
To those that love me
But, don't know my mind.

I long to be free,
For you to find me.
I long to find you,
As free as a bird.

We'd join together
Like a jigsaw that binds,
Freeing those pictures,
That torment my mind!

ELIZABETH BEVAN,
Nant-y-ffyllon, Maestege,
Mid-Glamorgan.

BETRAYED

You trampled my heart
Into the dust
Under your heels.
You never heard my screams
Of pain.
They were silent.

You discarded my soul,
Just threw away
What I gave
So freely, with such trust.
Such pain
Engulfing me.

I gave my love,
My heart, my soul,
All my passion.
You were perfect for me.
This pain
You left to me.

MARILYN BROOKS,
Llanrumney, Cardiff.

WINTER'S GRIP

The earth now solid as a rock.
All living things held in winter's unrelenting lock.
When frost at your fingers nip,
And birds cannot take a sip
From puddles smooth as glass
Transformed by Nature's icy blast,
Blows from the north.
And snow showers sally forth,

To chill and cover all in its wake,
And icicles hang waiting to break,
Waiting for the sun to melt
Soon in sheltered corners will be felt
Weak sunshine growing stronger,

With grey winter's day growing longer,
To herald the long awaited spring,
When the blackbird and thrush will sing.
And the snow drop and crocus will emerge
To signal Mother Nature's annual surge.

DOUGLAS DART
Topsham, Exeter,
Devon.

SMILE OF A CHILD

I have seen the sight of a setting sun,
   the wonderful thing of a life begun,
Felt the joy of a mother's love,
   looked from a hill at the stars above,
But nothing compares with the smile of a child,
   the innocent look, so undefiled,
The love they give with an open mind,
   nowhere on earth so much love will you find.
For a smile is all it has to give,
   with lots of love a joy to live,
But spare a thought for the child, where,
   there is nobody else to love and care,
For God meant us all to share,
   life's good gifts He gave us to bare,
When He gave us life on that first day,
   He said no one else would ever pay,
So let your heart go out to this child,
   who looked at you, held your hand and smiled.

CECIL B. CUNDELL,
Cambridge.

BIRTHRIGHT

The warm, wet, not quite rounded skull
the caul removed, like fragile lace.
A fierce pulsing sign of life, the fontanel;
pain and weariness visible on your face from
your rites of passage. Tiny fists
clenched like sea anemones, you already show
defiance to the world. For this
expulsion into clamour, light and cold:
you give no quarter. Your screams
fill up spaces in the room, you can't discern
that this is how it's meant to be. The seams
upon your troubled face will smooth
and instinct turns you to my breast, the scent of me
remembered from an already distant past.

CHRISTINE MARY DENT,
Scunthorpe, Lincolnshire.

ANYBODY THERE?

I haven't looked under a flower-pot since Bill and Ben.
But I can imagine the life that struggles beneath its curves.

Earthworms roll along, like moles, bulldozing the soil.
Snails stick to the chipped terracotta.
Rain assaults the circumference, and moss meshes on the vertical.

It brings back my childhood days,
When I inspected those square inches of ground, for signs of life.
Pushing and prodding at the tiny territory I'd discovered.

If I ever planted anything in that pot today,
It would be 'Rosemary' for remembrance.

JOAN M. EMMENS,
Melton, Woodbridge, Suffolk.

THE AWAKENING

No-one could wake her,
Though everyone tried.
The waking world had lost its fascination,
And the dreams seduced her
Till we could not bring her back.
We, too, grew weary;
The pain of our loss
Too great to bear with open eyes.
We wanted to be with her,
Wherever she was
And, tired at last
Of weeping, fell into sleep.
Who was it woke us?
Who first brought the news
Of our girl restored to us?
Not the girl we knew,
But one now fully aware.
Was it one more of her fantasies,
The pretty young man and his kiss?
Such a smile she sports
Came, surely, from more than this?

ELEANOR DENT,
Heath, Cardiff.

DON'T SET THE CLOUDS TOO LOW

Don't set the clouds too low -
    for dense the mists that veil my eyes
    and blur your image - sink your voice
    to indistinguishable tones;
    and memory in evanescent flight
    leaves me alone.

Don't set the clouds too low -
    I want to feel moonlight
    on cobbled streets, walk
    by your side, shelter
    in the warmth of your
    shadow as the solitary
    night deepens and plaintive
    lullabies echo a soulful
    yet uncertain quietude.

Don't set the clouds too low -
    I want to touch the stars -
    jewels on soft black velvet -
    so clear a sky; and for
    one fleeting moment
    in the dancing half-light
    recall you as you are
    and not as my doubtful
    memory would make
    you.

M. V. EASTWOOD,
Scunthorpe, Lincolnshire.

CLAIRE

Your mind is closed.
You can't understand.
What is life all about,
Why was this planned?

I love you Claire,
Your special features,
Your long dark hair.
Why was this planned?

Mental handicap is sad,
They blame both Mum and Dad.
But in your handicap I know
You still have a love to flow.

You sit and rock,
You scream and stamp.
But I love you still,
And Claire, I always will.

KARIN BEVERLY FIELD
Exeter, Devon.

REMEMBRANCE

Even though I can't see you
I know that you're there
You're the warmth in my heart
And the wind through my hair.

You know that I loved you
And am in pain now you're gone
You're the rain through the sunshine
And the notes in a song.

You weren't just a love to me
You were more than a friend
You were someone I could depend on
Right up to the end.

You were my confidante
My air when I couldn't breathe
You give me the courage
And strength to believe.

No other person
Could ever take your place
With your generous loving nature
And smile that lights your face.

No two other people
Will ever be a perfect match.

AMANDA J. FUDGE,
Pontypridd, Rhondda Cynnon Tâf,
Mid-Glamorgan.

THE LAKES IN WINTER

White-capped peaks, ice and snow
Wrapped-up hikers with a healthy glow
Fallen leaves on a wooded trail
Strong winds blowing a howling gale

Sun comes out and melts the snow
Tumbling water where rivers flow
All around an Alpine scene
Breathtaking beauty, an artist's dream

Waterfalls cascading from way up high
Floating pink clouds passing by
Stone built cottages in lonely places
Grazing sheep with jet black faces

Farmers toiling under a wintry sun
Soon heading home their day's work done
Windermere Lake and a steamer chugging by
A flash of wings from a bird in the sky.

An old coaching inn, greeting travellers late
With a roaring log fire in a big open grate
Brass plates hanging on an uneven wall
At that friendly inn, as I do recall

The lakes of Cumbria a spectacular sight
Reflections of a sunset heralding the night
Coniston, Elterwater, linger in the mind
Wonderful memories of a special kind.

BRENDA M. HADLEY,
Mapperley, Nottingham.

IN TOUCH

I still have his Cornish Pisky, brass and heavy with his feel,
Bought in Looe so many years ago.
Kept with his keys and used each day
And left to me.
I see now his old woolen dressing gown taken from the door,
Strong with scents of talc and sweat
And heavy with his life.
I sit and hold it to my face,
Inhaling him with every sobbing breath
And crying in the quiet now he's gone.
Stiffly I sit; lost in the funeral car, stiff and blank,
Shutting out mother, grieving family and friends.
Locked in navy blue school uniform with flowers in my eyes,
Their scent so strong they dye my mind,
Imprinting future flowers with that biting stain of grief.
Never more would I accept a gift of flowers without a tear
And flower shops intense with their perfume
Remain as funeral parlours in my mind.
I still possess my father though he died when I was young.
He lives inside my purse and in my head.
A smiling Cornish Pisky swinging on my keys
And the press of well-worn wool against my tears.

JANE WALLIS HICKS
Newport, South Wales.

LAST ACT

(for Ella, 1910 - 1996)

"Alis Volat Propiis"

You were not there, when last I saw you
As with unseeing eyes, you watched me stand before you,
It wasn't really you that lay, connected to the world today
But someone tired, world weary, weak and frail,
Fighting the close of life to no avail.
No! You were strong, and sure, and resolute in deed,
Defying life's misfortunes, mistress of the stronger breed,
How could I then stand by and watch you lie
Kept in a twilight world, while wishing just to die?
Mechanically functioning, yet gone from here
In all but hollow shell, on to a new frontier.
And so from deepest love, the die is cast,
Decisions made, you shall know peace at last,
Rejoining him with whom you shared a brighter day.
The deed is done, I hold your hand, you slip away.

PAUL J. THORNBER,
Castle Bromwich, Birmingham.

NO COBBLES NO CLOGS

Down the old cobble street, that I once knew,
The hand of friendship welcomed you,
A friendly greeting, a cheerful smile,
An invitation to stay awhile.
    No wealth or fortune did they possess,
    Yet life was so full of happiness,
    Never searching or asking a lot,
    Caring and sharing what they had got.
A street ful of laughter as children play,
This is their playground, every day,
Where children played in steel-soled clogs,
Whose dads kept pigeons and Greyhound dogs.
    The street that had memories, has now gone,
    Its houses demolished, one by one,
    Friends that were there, now drifted apart,
    To highrise flats, to make a new start.
Up in the world, the seventh floor,
Don't even know the neighbours next door,
When dad comes home at the end of his shift,
No walk down the street, but a ride in a lift.
    Modern times have changed the way they live,
    "Oh what", they say, "Oh what would we give
    To see our kids playing, in little clogged feet,
    Back in our dear old cobbled street".

THOMAS WALKER,
Ealand, Crowle, South Humberside.

MORTAL MEN

We are mortal men determining our terms,
like actors assuming many parts
in the theatre of our psyche.
What of love in weary hearts?
    Round and round in pointless races,
       filling up restricted spaces.
Spreading buttered toast with aromatic germs.

In the streets the rainbow lights of fairgrounds pledge.
Private lives dispence and keep,
silent voices cry out loud,
at honesty we laugh and weep.
    And round and round in breathless races,
       found in microscopic traces.
Torn between the chasm and the cutting edge.

Cruelty worn behind masks, too proud to wait.
On the threshold of a dream they shriek:
"The same above as below."
Bearing emblems of power we speak,
    concealing uncommitted crimes,
       in a chapter of our times.
With a voracious appetite, before the magistrate.

Our souls are voyagers who have no strength to rest.
Disordered public, stomachs fed,
form and colour break apart,
intense the palates painted red.
    The actor takes the part and mimes,
       for the chapter of our times.
We ride with triumph and we know we did our best.

JANE YATES,
Alkborough, Scunthorpe.

SEA SOUND

Slip slap, slip slap,
    sea on summer shore,
Jelly fish abandoned,
    not swimming as before.
Foaming fingers carelessly
    toss small shells around,
Creating a melodious,
    crunchy, clinking sound.

Boom crunch, boom crunch,
    Autumn seas are here
Playing "pitch and toss"
    with an empty can of beer,
Churning up the pebbles,
    spewing out the sand,
Exhilarating drum beats,
    echo round the land.

Crash thump, crash thump,
    heavy winter seas
Hurling up huge walls of ware,
    "Tanglers" to please,
Lashing out relentlessly
    at rubbish man throws out,
Heaving up fish boxes
    all with bottoms out.

Plop slush, plop slush,
    spring tides make their mark,
Seas reining in the fiendish sprites
    ready for a lark,
Sucking at the pebbles,
    spitting at the crags,
Softly washing debris
    from the Redstone flags.

PATRICIA M. SULLIVAN,
Eday, Orkney.

OBSERVATION

Did you see the rose unfold its petals to the world,
Or witness the birth of seeds as they emerge from the earth?
Have you listened to leaves telling secrets to the trees?
Maybe you were too busy
                      doing more important things.

Did you see the small face violets among decaying leaves,
Or witness the beginning of blossoms on winter's skeleton trees?
Have you listened to April showers tap dancing to the ground?
Maybe you were in a hurry
                      with no time to look around.

Did you see the ladybird try to balance on a mountain of grass,
Or witness a colony of worker ants on an organised march?
Have you listened to water trickling over diamonds of stone?
Maybe you were engaged
                      with trivial gossip on the phone.

Did you see snow and wind building walls of ice,
Or witness sun and rain making rainbows in the sky?
Have you listened to thunder fighting as lightning strikes?
Maybe you are one of the few
                      who observe Nature's many delights.

DAWN SHAW,
Cambridge.

MONEY

Such power in a word, the fruit of life,
Bringing joy or causing strife,
Addiction, obsession soon the wrath,
For all who chase along its path.
Child on child share the pain,
If brother, sister seem to gain,
He has more, she has less,
Money causing all the stress.
Not satisfied with what we need,
The balance tilted by the greed,
Though soon they all will come to know,
You spend it fast, you earn it slow.
Enjoy today, forget tomorrow,
See how much there is to borrow.
The common sense we seem to lack,
The struggle when you pay it back,
Yet if used wisely, taking care,
To teach the young ones how to share,
There'll be the money, less the strife,
And compassion as we go through life.

NICHOLAS A. RAY,
Kirton Lindsey, Lincolnshire.

SOLITUDE

Up, yonder, far as the eye can see,
There is a world of fantasy.
Where cloud and shadows fill our dreams,
Among the heather and mountain streams.
Where the air is fresh and bracken sweet,
And soft the feel of turf to feet.

The song of Skylark rises high,
Unending, upwards, to meet the sky.
Ferns, moving with the lightest air,
Wave welcome arms to bide you there.
While down in the valley far below,
The people hurry to and fro.

So high above, in Heaven's care,
The freedom of purest, freshest air.
In the valley dark shadows drop,
While sun pervades the mountain top.
Another world, so close to view.
Much nearer to the heaven's blue.

Is this the place to get away,
From all life's troubles, day to day,
And climbing higher to the peak,
Attain the solitude I seek.
A freedom found, a joy supreme.
Up here, upon the hill, I dream.

GYWNETH PRITCHARD,
Caerphilly, Mid-Glamorgan.

THE SKY

I relate to the sky
but what is it?

A vast dreamland filled with memories:
A silver-blue voyage to the stars,
A grey wasteland of despair,
A place where anger can roll
Like thunder,
Joy proposed by sunlight.
Clouds can be white and smile
or black and angry.

I relate to the sky
but what is it?

PETER NUTTALL,
Birtley, Co. Durham.

CONISTON WATER IN WINTER

I stood by a dazzling edge of water
Frozen in time and in light
Blue sheets of ice sighing
Heaving in a slow cold surge
Fractured, piling bright crystals on the shore
The sound of a thousand tinkling chandeliers
Set in a space of quiet
And surrounding sylvan hills.

Dr. DAVID CHARLES PEARSON,
Grange-over-Sands, Cumbria.

BRECKLAND WILDS

This rustic weave of Heathland's tapestry rare,
Of which languorous brooks and heather share
Vermillion sunset skies, as far as eyes can see,
With pale flavescent clouds floating gracefully,
Has given me such serene and gladsome days
Of awe-struck wonder for sweet Nature's ways.

This splendid motherland gifted by my God to me,
By birth and succour midst bracken'd brecks and lea,
Rich in its legacy of leafy forest, stream and mere;
And its soothing breeze with untainted vibrant air,
Is worth to me more than any enriched foreign turf
That mankind could find elsewhere on this Earth.

Aeons with changing climes have passed away
And bones of forefathers in sandy heath do lay,
A hidden wealth beyond thought of mortal man
Who has forgotten the heritage of this his land;
But I can feel the presence of my long past kin,
With every step I take in this land that I dwell in.

And if Death takes me to that enchanted place
Where I will meet the early founders of my race,
I'll reflect on joyful thoughts and wonders share,
As I speak to pagan folk of many legends there;
And hear beloved kin sing ancient Anglian songs
In ghostly brecks where my soul will ever roam.

MICHAEL K. MOORE,
Norwich, Norfolk.

Note: The East Anglian Breckland is an area of outstanding beauty. The brecks are ancient sandy heathland, abounding in bracken, gorse and ling with stunted birch, hawthorn and dwarf Scots pine. It is best seen in autumn when ridges, valleys, knolls and hollows are draped in the ghostly veil of early morning mist, or when a red sunset silhouettes the lonely stands of pine, casting long broken shadows over the wild landscape.

SEARCHING THROUGH LIES

There is poison in every cat's claws,
A maggot in every ripened apple.
Sickened trees shed their burden of leaves
like flakes of green skin.
They now stand naked brown and free,
yet dead,
Withered and unholy.
Forgotten twigs trod upon by swollen feet.
Lame legs stride over,
try to find their way
But it's impossible
In search of perfection
While life is full of deception.
Dolphins circle inside the sun.
Half-blinking, I see them turn round
and round,
Always anti-clockwise.
Their grey skins are rubber stretched,
Costumes of ridicule consuming the light.
The days used to be so bright
until the night came out to taunt
And downwards the mammals fell,
Their innocent child-like smiles lost
Inside blank glass fish eyes staring ahead.
People like to think they sleep safely in
their beds of feathers
Until the blood seeps through.
Who is killing who?
I think that when we blink a whole
Lifetime is missed.

LOUISE LUCAS,
Broxtowe, Nottingham.

BEAUTY-TRIGGERED CHAIN OF THOUGHT

There stands the tall Oak, its majesty a
Facade - not a spiritual blessing,
But a natural accident.
A series of chemical reactions
And tropic responses make forms with only
Terrestrial roots.

Rose from the abiotic and flourished in
Biotic privilege: to crumble in the
Empty cycle of elements.
Product of evolution - mutation and
Selection. Traced back to a single cell -
Born of the dust.

Yet, when was that time that dust took a breath?
Mark me the moment that dead was alive.
If genes mutate for survival,
Wht create such beautiful splendour that
Awes human minds which feel and think? When does
Dust become life?

Step back from the Oak tree, see a thousand
Oak trees swaying in the sweet breeze, strong arms
Outstretched proclaiming the Lord's worth.
Deep roots hold firm through the storms and the gales.
Glowing with spirit, radiating life!
Join with the trees.

AMANDA JAYNES,
Bamber Bridge, Preston.

PAGAN BEACHES

Under a northern star, on a Norwegian coast,
Outside of Verdal, through Trondheim up north.
Beneath mountains wild, it was Nature's child
That called my wandering spirit forth.

I walked without shadow from the midnight sun,
along endless silent miles of ragged coast,
by grey rocks and grey pines where the muskrat climb
and where grey seals slid by like grey ghosts.

That empty coast ran for a hundred miles
where black shags circled under a sky of grey tiles,
of scudding clouds, high in the glowing atmosphere
glaring down on the knife, rod and lonely man down there.

I walked those quiet endless miles of stones
with rod, knife and knapsack, and sat there alone
in my sealskin boots, under endless spreading skies,
grilled and ate my Coalfish, and just wondered why

There is no other need just like this endless wanting
to sit by a beach fire under that canopy of stars,
with a bright sky reflecting somebody else's daytime
throughout the still night up in Verdalsara.

TERENCE MICHAEL HOWE,
Brigg, Lincolnshire.

SPRING

Spring:
Awake, sleeping Mother Nature, awake!
Zephyr breeze stir the torpid form,
Lambent sunlight kiss the snowcap veneer.
Lustre of sequin droplets glisten
From tips of pendant icicle lances.

Spring:
Daffodil trumpets herald new season,
Narcissus, hearken sweet Echo, pining,
Summon fauna and flora from Nature's prison.
Woodland nymph and satyr lovers
Revel in Bacchanalian dance.

Spring:
Lovers gambol mid blue bell chimes,
Eros and Psyche in eternal tryst of intimacy,
O, sensual joy of creation Pasch.
Life to life consummate
A burgeoning of youthful spirit.

WILLIAM G. HEATLEY,
Scunthorpe, Lincolnshire.

LOVE

I looked to the east to see
The sun making love to the day.
The tiny glow grew fiery red,
Blushed, and warmed the earth,
Freed the secret smells of morning.

Russet leaves scuffled, crackled,
Lightly lifted to the breeze,
Fluttered to earth's heartbeat
And to the drumming of a lover's call,
Danced without warning.

The orange sphere, bright furnace
Of fire, slipped into the sky,
Primed the grey with carmine tint
And, like a secret brush of lips
Painted love's dawning.

MAY HAMILTON,
Atherstone, Warwickshire.

ON SILENT WING

The tawny owl on his deadly search
In ancient woodland of oak and birch,
He kills softly from noiseless flight,
The unheard hunter of the night.

The short-eared owl sweeps soft and low
Over the grasslands where the field voles go,
He deals in death in the afternoon,
Or in the pale light of the moon.

The long-eared owl stands stark and still
And waits for the moment when he must kill,
He hunts within the forest deep,
And takes his prey while others sleep.

The barn owl feeds on mouse and vole
And nests in hollow elm-tree bole,
He carries his prey at the dead of night,
Back to his lonely nesting site.

The owl - the bird of omen ill,
Who strikes into my heart a chill,
In the valley of darkness where he is king
Death comes swiftly - on silent wing.

GORDON GREY,
Yokefleet, East Yorkshire.

TO: 'LIFE'S CHILD'

*(After the death of an elderly woman found dying - alone -
from hypothermia, January 1997)*

You gave to her in death's cold repose, Life's Child, that
which you should have given to her in Life's warm home.

The cold that larked and played down corridor and passageways
froze the body full of numbered days and senses blurred
in thoughtless haze - through helplessness and confusion.

The aged ashes on the hard-baked hearth were crumbled, black and
grey, and full of dust. - No rosy, rosy glow of burning coals
to bid slow farewell to that poor, Life's Soul - bloodless
against the killing, bitter, bitter cold.

How well you speak of Souls, my Dear, when the body's flesh is dead;
and ply them well with conscience gifts instead. - Instead!
Aye! - Rake the coals to glow upon the hard-baked hearth, when
Soul and body move as one; and then the body's need is truly
done - in that cold room. Then: flex thy tongue with words -
full of compassion's grace, and settle with a simple smile upon
thy living face. - In satisfaction.

Sad! Sad! - Now, many, many flowers of brightly coloured blooms of:
pinks and reds, and yellows - of sweetened scent, fill to warm
the once cold and lonely room - now, as its tenant: a casket
tomb, with Souls gathered, dressed in Sunday-clothes of sombre
hues - a garland ring of unsweetened gloom, with tongues
mouthing deaf and fruitless words - in muted ballad song.

Sad! - Sad! - You called, dressed in Sunday's best - my Dear,
but: too late! - Too late! - That body's Soul has left
from here. - Fare thee well! - 'Life's Child'. -
Fare thee well.

WILLIAM G. THOMAS,
Shirley, Southampton.

DEAR SONG THRUSH

Ah, Speckled Song Thrush,
Does thine eye still shine
Within thy form, so still?
On winds of sorrows and sighings blown
My heart with thee to heaven is flown,
How should I call it down?
Thy feathers, lovely little thing,
Are deep beneath the ground.
They swooped between those cruel wheels
And fluttered and failed so soon,
And
Mangled now, my soul just feels
The horror that across their path still reels
To warn each passing wing.
I love thee, little sacred thing.
Though erstwhile I knew thee not,
I pray one day we'll meet again
And sing together some sweet refrain,
Safe from the dangers that here do reign,
Safe with the Father who rules o'er the main.
Then, secure in a friend's true pardon,
I'll stay with thee in God's garden.

MONA DRION,
Scunthorpe, Lincolnshire.

PAUSE A MOMENT

Pause a moment, stop a moment, rest a moment there,
Cease what you are doing, rest upon a chair.
You should have a moment, passing through each day,
So pause awhile, clear the mind, I'm sure this is the way.

You wake up in the morning, you hear the cockerel crow,
This is the signal for you, it means you have to go.
A little drink, a tiny snack, out in the morning crush,
To your work where'er it be, all in one hectic rush.

The business starts when you arrive, the pressure is now on,
Meeting costs and deadline times, or profits will be gone.
When your working time is done, and pleasure's on the way,
You're caught again in all the rush, to get to where you play.

Then when your pleasure is complete, and it's time now to return,
You drift back tired to your home, and watch the fire burn.
You may discuss with someone close, about your hectic day,
And hope they'll give you some advice, to keep you on your way.

Whilst you're having quiet talk, and partaking of a drink,
The peaceful moments you enjoy, will give you time to think.
You must recall what I first wrote, in my opening lines,
They will guide you on life's way, and help you read the signs.

Pause a moment, stop a moment, rest a moment there.
Cease what you are doing, rest upon a chair.
You should have a moment, passing through each day,
So pause awhile, clear the mind, I'm sure this is the way.

DONALD FUTER,
Bardney, Lincoln.

A CANDLE

Each time I light a candle
It's for someone alone,
Who's praying for a miracle
That never comes.
A spark of life
That burns so bright
To give them hope,
From my candlelight.

KIM T. BLUNDELL,
Manchester.

THE SWAN

Like a rugged coast and shore
'Tis you that I adore.
Like thunder in the sky I fear
I think of you and shed a tear.
Cygnets, oh so fluffy and grey,
Growing larger every day.
Arched necks meet entwined,
Elegance and beauty so refined,
With expert precision they build their nests
And ruthlessly attack unwanted guests.
A calm serenity so divine,
Peacefully sail the river of time.
The swan and family drift along,
Come the dawn, I find you've gone.
Oh, beautiful bird, don't fade away,
Live forever I hope and pray.

NICHOLAS FLETCHER,
Norton, North Yorkshire.

THE MISSED GOODBYE

You missed each other, he waved goodbye,
It was for ever; you did not see.
The bus moved forward with the day
Into a time of destiny.

You were no more than a silhouette
Climbing the stairs as he wished a glance;
But you did not look left or right,
You did not know, and missed the chance.

But do not feel sad you did not reply
As taken with others on life's bus.
We do not ring the stops of life
But those that stay will pray for us.

Although you were not to meet again
In some future time, your patient hand
Will feel the chance you missed in life
To wave hallo, and understand.

ALAN DICKSON,
Rochester, Kent.

TODAY FORGOTTEN

Wind is howling around my door,
The cold is creeping around my feet.
The night is longer than ever before,
Tomorrow again we'll meet.

Again today is nearly gone,
So soon to be forgotten.
Tomorrow will not be long,
But as soon to be forgotten.

Black night leaving now,
Soon to come the daylight.
Black night leaving now,
Goodbye the night.

Tomorrow is today,
Leaving us never.
What is tomorrow?
But echoes of forever.

NEVILLE HICKS,
Kendal, Cumbria.

THE LESSON

One only learns
Through personal experience
Time after time
You will get burnt
Until wisdom prevails
And the lesson is learnt.

KIM T. BLUNDELL,
Manchester.

SPRING

Snowdrops and crocus herald the Spring
Heads held high in the icy wind,
Carpeted like a blanket of snow
Their gentle heads sway in the breeze that blows.
Beautiful colours in the gardens bright
In hues of purple, gold and white,
What pleasure they bring to young and old
Showing us how the seasons unfold.
Gamboling lambs in the farmer's field,
Hedges and trees new buds they yield.
Sunshine to follow the shower of rain
That patters on my window pane.
Time will move on and the seasons unfold
To welcome the Summer in a blaze of gold.
That is how our seasons unfold.

CORWENA JONES,
Walton le Dale, Preston.

APPRECIATING AUTUMN O'ER CROMARTY FIRTH

In Autumn, there is just one kind
of picture painted in my mind.
The changing colours of the leaves
through frost and sun and chilly morning breeze:
The never-ending beauty of it all,
beckons me with strong and silent call.
Though this path I'll travel o'er on many days,
I'm yet content with Nature's wondrous ways.

Autumn has a language of its own;
calming my despair when I'm forlorn.
The magic changing colours of the leaves
whisper me their secrets in the breeze.
The Autumn sun, reflecting o'er the Firth,
shines like gold - which glows in all its worth.
The tide is out and Nature's in abound.
Once again, I hear Nature's sweetest sounds.
Avenues of Nature's greatest gifts;
- in Autumn fall; - my spirits lift!

ROSEMARY A. V. SYGRAVE,
Bristol.

MY IMAGINATION

My imagination is precious to me;
It's a comforting friend when I am lonely.
And while I lie asleep in bed,
My imagination creates a whirl inside my head.
Sometimes my imagination gives me a scare
By creating a horrible gloomy nightmare.

Maybe tomorrow, dear imagination, we'll go and visit Mars,
or Pluto, or Saturn, maybe sit among the stars.
Or, leap up tall buildings like Spiderman;
With your help, I know that I can.
My imagination lets me dream that I am on TV,
Or that I have won one million pounds on the Lottery.

My imagination lets me see
That I can be anyone I want to be.
Or, do anything, or be anywhere;
It makes me feel that I am walking on air.
My imagination creates a magic show,
That sets my very heart aglow.

No tricks or illusions needed you see;
It's just my imagination, my friend and me.
I love to dream the day away;
Allowing my mind to gently stray,
Pretending that I am a queen,
Or an actress, performing a romantic love scene.

Now I am being rocketed into space;
And when there is a problem, I am always on the case.
When I am sad, I just think of you;
Thank you, my imagination, you are a friend who is
                                            loyal and true.

NINA ABEL, aged 14 years.
Totton, Southampton.

LIGHTS, CAMERAS, ACTION!

A slap on the back,
A pat on the head,
Don't forget to play dead.
Here is your script,
You are here,
Don't forget to look queer.
You in a minute,
You now!
Don't forget the costume cow.
This is great!
Tomorrow's the date.
Lights, Cameras, Action!

ALEX HERDMAN, aged 10 years (now 14 years)
Waterbeach, Cambridge.

AUTUMN DAYS

Autumn is coming,
Under the leaves the hedgehog is asleep.
The plants are dying and turning different colours.
Unstopping rain pours on our windows.
More puddles create in hollows.
Now we can splish and splosh in them.
Days are short, nights are long.
Animals gather food for the winter.
You can see them in the woods.
Some people like autumn, some don't.

DAVID QUINNELL, aged 9 years.
Hazlemere, Bucks.

DREAMLAND

I dream of a world where I can fly
I dream of a world in upper realms of my mind
I re-enact thoughts with a million different scenes
I lay the seeds for magic beanstalks with very magic beans

My mind caresses my heart as well as my soul
Creating perfect harmony in a world that can be cruel
My dreams are full of wonder and questions to answer
And knights in shining armour killing dragons with lances

To some people a dream is just a dream it seems
A part of their mind that opens its screens
But to me a dream is much much more
Another dimension, another life, an open door

Could it not be that our dreams are for real
Instead of this life where we need food as fuel?
In this mystical land I don't need food nor drink
I just use my mind to move as I think

The power of being is there to be taken
Just hold out your hands and prepare to awaken

GLENN McKENZIE,
Bramcote, Nottingham.

ENLIGHTENED

Where is the Man awakened? Who is he,
Who is as all men alive should be,
Whose daily life, whose every act and thought
Is with high aim and conscious purpose wrought?
By patient ways he has a length attained
To know himself; and deeper understanding gained
In some degree of that great Cosmic Plan
Which calls the service of Awakened Man.
With wider knowledge much is now to him revealed
Which to our clouded minds is still concealed,
His self is freed of our mechanic ways and thought
Of earthly fears and doubts and minds distraught
Outward, quiet calm and peace; within, a shining light
Making all men, all things, to seem in One unite.
This, then, the vision; have we a chance like him to be?
Then must we work in hope that we, too, this light can see.

GEORGE A. LEE,
Lepton, Huddersfield.

FIELD OF DREAMS

As you close your eyes, allow the breeze of the night to sway you towards the sea of tranquility. Bathe in the light of the everlasting flame, as you absorb the wisdom of the universe. Drift slowly and gently into the arms of Morpheus as you enter the field of dreams.

JOHN GRIFFITHS,
Solihull.

CAERPHILLY OF YESTERDAY

Caerphilly once a quiet town,
A gentle tranquil country place
With a castle on a mound.

Few people knew this haven,
Only famous for its cheese,
Where everyone was friendly
And always at their ease.

How things have changed, I'm sad to say,
The quiet times have gone away
And turmoil reigns in this sad town,
Where everything is upside down.

They've razed the buildings to the ground
And torn the heart from this small town.
It's called progress, so they say.
Oh, please bring back yesterday,
When life was normal and we felt sane
And daily life was far less strain.

GLORIA THOMAS,
Caerphilly, Mid-Glamorgan.

LISTENING

Showers of flowering notes
Purify with joy and tears.
The bow-charmed violin sings
While the mourning cello weeps.
A silver cataract tumbles from the flute
And an oboe yearns with poignant tone.
Heralding horns demand attention,
Kettle-drums echo a primal sonority,
And the metal petals of percussion
Ring in exultation.

JOAN McCLUNG,
Norden, Rochdale.

THE ROCKING HORSE

Backwards and forwards - a rattle and a creak -
What happens at night when grownups are asleep?

As darkness shrouds the edges of the room,
Through criss-crossed panes a moonlight's ray
Spotlights much merriment in the gloom
As little people laugh and play.

Chuckling, chortling, giggling, with delight
On the willing rocking-horse they climb,
Joyful pixies, merry elves - a trifle tight
From nectar, having a good time.

Backwards and forwards - a rattle and a creak -
This is what happens when grownups are asleep!

NYARI JOY NORTH,
Kendal, Cumbria.

BLESSINGS

When you're feeling low
And don't know what to do -
Just go and sit down quietly
And take a good look at you.

Are'nt you really lucky
Compared to many, many more?
You have your food and clothing
And your very own front door.

The hymn says, "Count Your Blessings",
Yes, count them one by one.
You really will be quite surprised
At what the Lord has done.

IRENE KELSEY,
Sutton Coldfield.

FORGOTTEN JOURNEY

Across the cloudless sky, a vapour trail
That marks the path of mighty, metal bird,
White against cerulean ground, a ribbon tail,
For a while remains and then is softly blurred.
A distant journey's indicator, a floating sign,
Slowly disappears, a fading, merging line.

A single life sails by and in its wake
Drift memories of events, of words and deeds,
Filling one with sweetness or a dulling ache.
Gradually, in due course, remembrance recedes.
Concepts and images, the passing years suppress;
Dreamlike, in seas of time, they sadly evanesce.

JOAN McCLUNG,
Norden, Rochdale.

SONG OF THE SILVER STAR

Twinkle, twinkle little star
Oh how beautiful you are
Shining bright within my eye
Without colour or symmetry,
Mystics search you far and wide
Across the Gulf, the Dark Divide,
Never knowing that they keep
The Pearl of Wisdom hidden deep
Within their Soul, the hidden house of IAO.

And from the Spheres arise again
The Songs of Love of ancient friends
Renewed again by Death and Birth
Until all those who hear them know
The wondrous music in their Soul,
The hidden house of IAO.

Friends and lovers meet once more,
Their meeting opens up the door
To memories of forgotten lives
We lived in love of IAO.

The Books we left behind are clues
To those we know and those we knew,
To those who know the 93,
The Perfect Love, agapé,
Shining deep within your Soul
The secret house of IAO.

ROBERT E. TASKER-POLAND,
Heol-Y-Cyw, Bridgend,
Glamorgan.

ADDICTED

The craving still with me
The pain was so sweet
With feeling still burning
An aching to meet
Resistance is over
Deep longing to quell
Addiction is screaming
You know that so well
I fought long and hard
To escape from this snare
But your voice had me running
Right back to your lair
You're breaking my heart
And yet cleansing my soul
Destroying my being
While making me whole
Your word still commands me
But the sting in the tail
Is that sweetest of poisons
That makes my strength fail.

NOELLE WORSLEY,
Sidmouth, Devon.

INCARNATE

The dent in our bed where he has lain
Is like an abyss to my unsleeping brain;
Where once was a warm and sensual being,
There is an empty space, painful, unforgiving.

Nights are lonely now he has gone;
When our love for each would climax as one.
How I ache for the touch of his fond embrace;
God knows the reason why he died apace.

But he did not die - he fell asleep,
Never to wake from that enduring sleep.
No loving kisses, no goodbyes, he was tired
He said, "Just to rest" - but his life expired.

As I knelt to loose his hand from mine,
He 'smiled' in submission, so supine.
Two tears had sprung from unseeing eyes;
His parting gift I supped in kissing guise.

My hands they sought to feel once more
His masculine form, I was so sure
He would respond, but his soothing balm
Had stilled within a spiritual calm.

If I could reach his bless'd eternal state;
If I could rise up and embrace my mate;
Then might I lose the haunting of my brain
And dissolve away this endless pain.

JENNIFER WRIGHT,
Kendal, Cumbria.

NICOLA'S BABY

Lovely little one
With so much black hair,
(Like your mother's before you) -
And early into this world!

Lying there, helpless and sweet,
One tube fixed to hand,
Another inside nose -
But fast asleep!

Such small hands,
Tiny fingers, and nails -
Long legs kicking in the air,
Unladylike!

Right eye tightly shut,
Left eye half-open,
Yet alert to one's touch
Through the open 'peep-holes'
In the 'funny cot' - like a boat!

Red face and limbs,
A few bruises, still,
Pretty mouth and lips, and -
Little yellow nose!

Content though, and warm,
Perhaps cosy, too?
Hardly a murmur, yet,
As if still in the womb?

Dear Katie Louise,
So glad you've arrived,
Even early contrived!
Surrounded by Love,
You're sure to survive.

SHEILA J. WILSON,
Upper Poppleton, York.

A ROLLER COASTER RIDE

Deceiving start. A gentle ride.
All safe, secure and calm inside,
Chatter, laughter, with thrills ahead,
Sedately glide, then downward sped.
Abrupt the change, as up we climb,
Now downward rush, we scream this time.
Faster still to reach a hollow,
Pulses race, we shout and bellow.
Racing higher, all laugh with fright,
Rush down again, now holding tight,
Wind blows the hair, chokes back the scream,
Defying death, nightmare and dream.
One moment laughs, next minute fears,
Gripped knuckles, white, eyes full of tears,
So gently up, more slowly down,
This last small climb, the final crown.
Cheers of relief, we deftly glide,
End of the Roller Coaster ride.
Feet safely now on solid ground,
Rejoin the throng and noisy sound.

AQUILLA,
Tunbridge Wells, Kent.

THE VISION

How stately she glides
Her skirts feathered wide.
All dressed in white,
A beautiful bride.
Water music gently played,
As proudly she moves
Through the leafy glade.
All nature's glories to the fore.
Where from this vision?
I declare, a Swan, it was,
I saw!

SARAH ROBINSON,
Pakefield, Suffolk.

THOUGHT FOR TODAY

If you really believe all you've been taught
Perhaps in your mind should linger the thought
Of loved ones departed who watch from above
Whose only desire is to shower you with love,
To guide and protect you in waking and sleeping
But what do they see while their vigil they're keeping,
Do they see the kind, true friend they once knew,
Or are they seeing now the dark side of you,
A side which perhaps, during their life was hidden?
Do you tread a path now which they may have forbidden?
Whichever it be, think hard, think deep
From those loved ones, dark secrets, you no longer can keep,
So think of the image you now portray
In the eyes of loved ones watching o'er you today,
Change course if need be, take steps to amend
Before the time comes when you'll meet them again.

DAVID BLANEY,
Loftus, Cleveland.

THE FOREST

Shadows coyly flit o'er dappling fronds,
Ne'er aware of beauty nature didst a'glean;
Such fine display for those who stand
In breathless wonder of a scene
No painted canvas couldst recapture, true;
The wonders there-portrayed for me and you.

Trees of towering majesty sublime, ensue
To reach aloft and kiss a sky of azure blue,
With cotton-candy clouds adrift,
Extending tendril fingers from above,
To sweet-caress the soaring realms of leafy green;
Touch thereupon as lovers, couldst be seen!

Diamonds could inferior-be to rippling streams
That vainly shine, akin to twinkling stars at night;
The depths extolling fleeting rays of warming sun!
Couldst a soul then gaze upon more wondrous content,
Than paradise, which sprinkled o'er by angel dust;
Perhaps be deemed as straight from heaven sent?

Hither and thither, twixt the leafy columns tall;
Swift of wing, with wondrous sound,
The birds of multi-coloured hue do joyous sing,
Proclaiming-they their praise of nature all around!
Wouldst it not-be honest then, to full-embrace
With thanks, for such a glorious place?

Tho' angels strive to magnify such glory;
The more to fine-enhance such painting there afore;
'Tis God alone who wields the brush
And lays the final touch 'pon canvas there!
Could it be, that even angels smile to fair-recall
Such works of art, which are displayed for one and all?

DENNIS F. TYE,
Norwich, Norfolk.

GOD'S WORLD

God's world is meant to be
Full of joy and love, you see;
But through the years as
Time goes by,
You'll see people laugh,
You'll see people cry.
In times of trouble,
In times of pain,
You'll learn to love
And care again,
For God has made this
World, you see,
For everyone,
For you and me.

LINDA SHEPPARD,
Tonyrefail, S. Wales.

CHARITY

We are all not wise
In the ways of this world,
Impulsive and lacking in clarity;
But remember what the good book says,
Our saving grace is charity.
Without it we are nothing,
With it we are all;
And if we play our true part,
We need not fear the call.
Our sins may be forgiven,
For even though we have erred,
Our hope lies in the very fact,
We did show that we cared.

WILLIAM DOCKER,
Perry Barr, Birmingham.

SNOW

The sky is grey and heavy laden.
The air is still. The Earth lies stiff,
Bracing itself for an icy winter covering.
Quietly, gently the snowflakes fall.
They blanket overall in pristine whiteness,
Transforming flower and tree and all things stationary
Into a three-dimensional scene of endless waiting.
No birds sing.

Eventually, the sun appears, a golden glow
Is spread around, and glistening sparklets
Dance above the ground.
We cast our shadows where we carefully are treading.

Children press eager faces against the schoolroom glass.
They cannot wait to build that snowman or
Whiz past the teacher's hat, with soft ball of snow.
Soon their voices ring clear as they slide or glide
Down a grassy slope,
Or fall with heavy thud, then helped aloft again.
They reduce the white, to shades of grey.
The snow is not so tempting now.

Across the way, where whiteness still remains,
A cheeky robin, searching in vain for crumb
Of cake or bun,
Leaves arrows where his feet have been.
Tomorrow will be different
When the snow has gone.

DOREEN COX,
Balsham, Cambridge.

OUR WORLD

So many people nowadays
Have no God to pray and praise -
How do they think the Earth began
With seas and land - and then came Man?

How did the acorn become an oak?
How did cities spring up with folk?
Why is the Bible the best loved book?
Where came the rivers, the rippling brook?

The world is full of hate and strife.
Rarely today do husband and wife
Keep the vows they made in the Hose of God
And follow the path the Saviour trod.

Pandora's box was opened wide;
The ills within, they multiplied.
But we had not the sense to see
That hope and truth were there for free.

If only we could learn to pray
For God's help from day to day.
What a different world this would be
With war and strife a memory.

Now love and peace will pave the way
For happiness to cheer each day.
The world will be a better place
With faith, perhaps we'll see His face ...

The Lord of every living thing
Of fish and beasts and birds that sing,
Of sun and moon and stars at night
Of beauty that is infinite.

INEZ M. HENSOM,
Leicester.

SUMMER

Lazy days when the sun is high
The breeze a whisper, just a sigh.
Giving momentum to the trees
A thousand and one honey bees.
Lonely, the kestrel way up high,
Swiftly swoops when prey is nigh.
Roses, whose perfect symmetry
Was not formed by you or me.
Tulips, who like sentinels stand
Guarding this our precious land.
Buttercups, yellow as sun at noon,
Lift the heart; dispel all gloom.
Golden hours and golden days
Burning heat; a distant haze.
The sweetness of the blackbird's song,
For this I yearn the winter long.
Summer storms, with clouds of rain
Soothe the anguished earth again.
Honeysuckle that perfumes the night,
Birds so swift, so true in flight.
Eventide, when the sun sets low
Kindling the sky with its fiery glow.
Clouds are scorched, they turn to flame,
Is such beauty all in vain?
Time is short, we are not free
To linger in this ecstasy.
These golden days, too soon, are gone
And we are left, oh, so forlorn.
Yet Nature's joys are ever there
For those who pause to stand and stare.

SIMMONE DOLBY,
Sawston, Cambridge.

VAGRANT MEMORY

Beneath the eyes of darkness,
Faintly, echoes the cries for help
But no hand is reached out,
Only the sense of doubt.
Do we trust a heart so poor,
Or, are we the untrusting ones.
We have let him down before,
Do we let him down again,
Or somehow ease the pain?
A face that has lived a thousand dreams
Now survives to live at all.
The fruitful past is just a memory.
Worn hands that search for scraps to eat,
The unwashed face is now down-beat,
Yet, no hands reach out to him.
We only look and stare
And walk on by without a care.
He laughs off all the hurt and pain,
As he sits beneath the pouring rain.
The eyes of darkness close for night
And still the cries for help are heard.
When you relax and day is done,
Just remember this is someone's son.
Did you reach out your hand?

SEAN PHELEN,
Billesley, Birmingham.

THE SUN OF MAN

We both hang suspended
Between the earth and sky.
You in ferocious beauty,
Drab specks of dust, I.

Men's million generations
will have known your face;
I may pass by unnoticed
Amongst the human race.

Yet my world is the greater
Than you will ever know;
For I have care and compassion
And love before I go.

Hurtling through the heavens
When life on earth is done;
Who will love you, then
When all of us are gone?

You will remain in limbo
Slowly getting cold;
In Stygian desolation
Lingering, growing old.

HELEN HAMPTON,
Crediton, Devon.

PUFFINS SIT UPON THE ROCKS

Puffins sit upon the rocks
With their heads held high.
They ponder the rythm of the waves
And watch the world flow by.
They sit and seem oblivious
To the cacophony of sound
And the ever-shifting movement
Of their neighbours settling down.
With their small, black-white bodies
And their bright coloured bills,
Stoically they sit there
Facing into ocean chills.
Hypnotised by the motions,
Entranced by dancing beams
They settle thinking puffin thoughts
And dreaming puffin dreams.

LYNDA NEWCOMBE,
Thornhill, Southampton.

IMAGINATION

Pluck the rosy-red apple and imagine the maggot inside:
Picture the deckchair sleeper and imagine the incoming tide:
Gaze on the yellow laburnum and imagine the poison within:
Smile at the welcoming stranger and imagine the breast-laden sin:
Gather a bouquet of roses and imagine the thorns 'neath their heads:
Listen awhile to the stories and imagine the dark-nurtured dreads:
Draw close to the comforting fire and imagine flame-seared skin:
Greet the suave, cloaked Count and imagine his blood-soaked grin:
Plunge into the crystal water and imagine the current's dire force:
Admire the noble jungle cat and imagine the flesh-tearing claws:
Consider the romantic courtship and imagine the pain of deceit:
Coo at the Spring lamb frisking and imagine the abbatoir bleat:
Bask in the celestial flame-orb and imagine the cell-splitting foe:
Think of the wondrous mushroom and imagine the vapourous glow:
Sleep in the satin bedchamber and imagine the nightmare's bite:
Enjoy the rich foods of the gods and imagine the underleaf blight:
All these arrayed for our thoughts and spoiled by imagination.

FRANCES G. DELANEY,
Westcliff, Scunthorpe.

DESPAIR

Inch by inch along the tightrope
I cross life's great divide,
Please, won't someone help me
I can't reach the other side.
On my right lies harsh reality,
My left tranquility.
Suspended in the mist of fear
With eyes that will not see
Grief is locked within me,
No solace can I find.
Tearless, soundless sorrow
Trapped in the turmoil of my mind.
Names upon my lips -
Memories echo in my head
Wish they were here to guide me,
Not in the valley of the dead.
But should I slip and stumble,
My body plunging through the air,
Would I be afraid?
No, I would not care.
Past loves would enfold me,
Bear my spirit to the skies.
They would not ignore me,
Turn a deaf ear to my cries,
Yet I take another step
Seeking solid ground,
One of life's lost souls
Yearning to be found.

GLENYS PRIEST,
Barry, South Glamorgan.

THE 13th OF OCTOBER

It rains hard today.
When we first met, the frost sparked shining
on paths and steel sides of cars.

We agreed, this day, the 13th of October, would be ours;
however we'd become or not become.
We'd meet by the afternoon square, rain or no.

Perhaps you have forgotten, but I
(being, as you know, of elephant memory)
let nothing slip by unnoted. The 13th of October
it is; the hard slanting wetness against the walls
and dappled sides of houses falls today.

The sky drops sharp pellets, heavy and icy, at my scalp.

The square holds single cowering shapes
under wide umbrellas,
specks of colour to its dark corners.
The steps of the clock-tower care no more than I
how high the rain bounces against them.

I wait for you regardless,
knowing that you will not come,
knowing that I can say: I did.

I was here when it came, the 13th of October, rain or no.

Then I go.

It doesn't matter, I say. It doesn't matter.

SONIA LOUISE OVERALL,
Canterbury, Kent.

TODAY

The snowdrops are hardly here,
But still the sun appears,
Now I awaken to the light and birds,
But these are only words,
Nothing compares to this dream of renewed faith,
Chased away the winter of hate,
The daffodil is yellow not blue,
It's growing and here for you,
Reminds me this is enough,
The nature of love.

ALISON WINFIELD,
Littleover, Derbyshire.

THE NEW LIFE

Just a heartbeat in a blind world
Of a mother's womb, resting and awaiting to unfurl.
An attempt to waken God's gift to man;
To make way from a peaceful plan.
A life waiting for this seed of life,
To storm the world that is full of strife.
Why does our Maker give us this start?
This painful thrust into life to impart.
The silence that was theirs now broken;
Noises and the new words spoken;
Awakens a mind that must now start to learn
The hardships in life and never to return
To the warm haven that was its forepart,
Until the day our Lord says it is time to depart.

VALERIE MARSHALL,
Scunthorpe, Lincolnshire.

LEGACY

The lush bank rises, steep and high,
Across the crest the spirits fly.
Long dead minds sigh and see
The waste that was so hard to meet.

Catalogues of terror - plain and stark,
Pain and fear, clean and sharp.
Falling on to the glistening blades,
"Tut tut", say the safe ones: "Such a shame."

The new green dappled with oceans of red.
Under the soil they're never dead.
So we can be what we want now
They gave it all and felt so proud.

Crawling like vermin: "Find a hole!"
The steel rain flashes and plays its role
In this terrible game - a game of death,
The mud and blood stained final breath.

The ones who choked on iron and mud
Live on forever, in my love.
And because this waste is never right
My sons will have their wars to fight.

ADRIAN MANNING,
Orpington, Kent.

A SUMMER'S DAY

A blackbird sings from the distant trees
As butterflies dance on a summer breeze,
The roses scent the hot, dry air
While bees collect the nectar there.
A sparkling pond reflects the light
Where koi carp fish show colours bright.
The fuschias hang their heavy heads
And colour cascades in the pansy beds.

The golden sun that lights the sky
With thermal winds where swallows fly,
Rich-leafed trees that shimmer green
Where fledglings learn to fly unseen,
A day when Nature's treasures glow,
Her richest colours now she'll show,
A distant sound of children's play,
The magic of a summer's day.

Not for me a barren land
When Winter shakes his frosted hand,
Sending snowflakes swirling round
Covering white the frozen ground.
So, when I leave this earth I pray
That it will be on a summer's day,
While my frame is warmed by the sun above
As my soul ascends to join those I love.

JANET MORTON,
Winterton, Lincolnshire.

TELEPHONE LINES

I lift the phone and hear you smile
As you say "Hello" to me;
And though you are so far away,
So close you seem to be.
Your voice is a bridge that reaches out
Across the land and sea,
Joining us together
Until you are home with me.
Until then, my Darling,
The phone will keep us close;
But some things it cannot do,
The things that I miss most:
It cannot let me hold you,
Or feel your loving touch,
Your strong arms wrapped around me
I miss so very much.
But one day soon, my Darling,
You will be home to stay
And in your arms I'll soon forget
You ever were away.
Until then, there is one thing
The telephone can do,
It can let me hear those precious words
When you say, "I love you."

PAMELA EVANS,
Maesteg, Mid-Glamorgan.

A HANDFUL OF COLOURS

In corridors of narrowness,
I hear foreign words confess,
The cracks of ware,
Shutters shut, open to stare,
The rusty bell,
Sounding to the leathery smell,
Brightly coloured flowers everywhere,
Guitar plucked in air,
Archways so tall,
Avenues run and run to small.
So proud he sits outside,
Thinking, watching it go by.

ALISON WINFIELD,
Littleover, Derbyshire.

SONNET: DROPS OF RAIN

Pendulous, fluid jewels glistening,
Suspended gems along balcony rail.
Tremulous globules shimmering, sparkling,
Refracted light - rainbow hues creating,
Gently, wind-wafted, they're yet not shifting;
Transient, inestimable riches
Arrayed out there. Now craftily breeze-caught
- Wobble precariously - now displaced -
Plummet to earth like leaden meteors,
Or, splattered into air like lemon zest.
Identical drops replace their fellows;
Miniature chandeliers dazzling the eye.
The sun who shows their beauty is their end.
End is steaming, drying board; gems - all gone.

VIVIENNE ROSCOE,
Rowell, Milnthorpe, Cumbria.

THE UNIVERSE AND I

I aim to reach the sun,
Propelled by my dreams:
Wings of Icarus.

Sometimes I perceive
That I'm as near as Mercury.
Occasionaly created
Is the vision that
I'm as distant as Pluto
From achievement in life.

Time passes:
My life and feelings change
As I hop from one planet to another.
I do not remain
On any one planet, for longer
Than one revolution of The Earth.
Neither do I
Make gradual progression
Or consistent regression
In my quest for the orb of day.

Sometimes I float
In open space:
My mind pondering on alternative thoughts.

Eventually I plunge
To the reality of Earth
Where tranquility is to discover
Day to day fulfilment:
Regardless of the planet
Or distance from the glow.

TRISTAN HARRIS,
Northfield, Birmingham.

INSOMNIA

Velvet darkness
Black as a raven's wing.
A leaden silence,
Sullen sleep suspended
Loth to yield to nature's need.

Far off and faint
A solitary owl
Calls from a ghostly tree.
Silence again.
Time like a tortoise
Limps on its languid way.
A passing plane drones
High above the clouds,
Bound for a distant land,
While sleep, the siren, beckons
Playing hide-and-seek.

Thoughts buzz in the head
Like bees in lavender.
Limbs shuffle restlessly,
Eyes long for sleep.
Yet sleep, evasive as a butterfly
Sulks in the shadows.

The minute hand creeps round the dial.
Time crawls as slowly as a funeral hearse,
And with the dawn there comes a gentle breeze.
Day breaks and weary eyelids find repose.

MARGARET BALL,
Exeter, Devon.

DEAREST TREASURE

You are my heart's desire,
My imagination a burning fire.
True to you I'll always remain,
Feelings of love so hard to contain.
Oh! Valentine, my dearest treasure,
My love is yours for ever and ever.

To embrace would be my delight,
Creating stars of joy so bright.
How alluring you always seem,
Captivating me as I dream.
Oh! Valentine, my dearest treasure,
My love is yours for ever and ever.

This love of mine so pure and true,
Darling, I bequeth to you.
Cards and roses sent as a token,
Spell words of love silent not spoken.
Oh! Valentine, my dearest treasure,
My love is yours for ever and ever.

JEAN M. OSBORNE,
Ashbourne, Derbyshire.

RAIN THROUGH A WINDOW

Like tears
Trickling down a soft cheek,
The rain gently falls
In rivulets,
Misting the windows.
As if one was looking
Through tear-filled eyes.

SARAH ROBINSON,
Pakefield, Suffolk.

HONEYSUCKLE SCENT

Honeysuckle scent, honeysuckle scent,
a sweet rich honeyed perfume,
a scent that's only lent.
In the summertime it permeates
in the wind that gently blows
the scent around the garden
and through the house it goes,
to drift around the house,
sweet-smelling honeysuckle scent.

Honeysuckle scent, honeysuckle scent,
the sweetness of such flowers,
a scent that's only lent.
On a summer breeze it lingers,
to attract the honey bees,
such a sweet-scented flower,
Oh, sweet honeysuckle breeze.

JAN MARSTON,
Leicester.

WINTER

Winter is a sad time
When all the earth is still
And everything is waiting
For the sunshine o'er the hill

But the hills and dales are silent
Beneath the snow so deep
And everyone is waiting
For the aconite to peep

The snowdrop is the first flower
To brave the winter's chill
Swiftly to be followed
By the golden daffodil

The ponds and dykes are frozen
Beneath the ice so cold
And everyone is waiting
For the crocus to unfold

And when the springtime comes along
With soft refreshing rain
I thank God for everything
And life begins again.

COLIN MUSSON,
Welbourn, Lincolnshire.

THE OAK TREE

Planted long ago
After the winter's snow
The acorn grew.
Fresh shoots so new.
Its branches grasp the sun
Reaching closer for fun.
Now stands noble and supreme,
A giant, it does seem.
Looks down upon the world
As passing seasons are unfurled
Offers shelter to creatures great and small.
Any weary traveller will find a seat,
Especially in the midday heat.
Forests crashing, such falls.
No more eagle's calls.
The cuckoo is far over due.
The mistle thrush is not on cue.
A nightingale is rarely heard.
But through time elapsing
And nature collapsing
The oak tree still stands,
Proud to be part of our lands.

PATRICIA MACPHERSON,
Brampton, Cumbria.

SOMEONE TO TAKE THE BLAME

Somewhere in the darkness
A tortured spirit cries;
A soul which longs for freedom,
Away from these foul skies.
A person can have no rest
When conscience begins a war,
And guilt, it has no mercy,
Even the pure can sleep no more.
The guilty don't always feel it,
This conflict in the mind;
And those who may be blameless
Can leave sanity behind.
This spirit with a secret
That haunts the dead of night,
May never find its peace
Nor distinguish wrong from right.
The right that they committed
Hurt someone else's pride,
And now they have to suffer
From confusion deep inside.
Some people are very selfish
And like to shift the blame.
Whilst others, they are trodden on -
Too honest to play the game.
I pray for the troubled one
That one day their sun will shine.
I hope this for all humanity
And because it's a soul like mine.

YVETTE DAY,
Carrington, Nottingham.

THOUGHTS

A newborn baby gives some lusty cries,
An old man weeps before he dies.
We are here on this earth to live all our life
With sadness and joy, happiness and strife.

Live your life, enjoy every day.
Be kind to others and sometimes pray
For the homeless and loveless, the hungry and sad
And though you don't want to, forgive the bad.

Appreciate beauty, the trees and the flowers.
Take time with your children and remember the hours
You've loved them, kissed them and wiped all their tears
For you'll have these memories at the end of your years.

All things must pass, as someone once said.
How true that is, for soon you'll be dead,
Gone like the wind on a brisk Autumn day
But you'll be remembered in your own special way.

MAXINE AINGE,
Preston, Lancashire.

DREAMING

Day dreaming, dozing, drifting,
Through the passages of time.
Remembering and reliving,
The memories that I find.

Memories of days gone by,
When we were only children.
Recalling sounds and smells and things,
And toys we played with then.

Whips and tops and skipping ropes,
Are very rarely seen,
Hop Scotch, marbles, chequers, gone.
As the Maypole on the green.

Remembering the clean fresh smell,
Hay drying in the summer's air.
Mixing with the meadowsweets' scent,
Making perfume rich and rare.

An aeroplane's drone up in the sky,
Brought us running to the street.
The musical song of the sky lark,
Her nest in the meadow, at our feet.

Day dreaming, dozing, drifting,
As the mists of time roll by.
Letting us relive our childhood
And the days long since gone by.

JOAN JEMSON,
Brotton, Saltburn-By-The-Sea,
Cleveland.

SECURITY

Sitting alone at my desk
Just thinking of you,
Music playing softly in the background,
My pen flows over the page.
This cosy, happy, peacefulness,
It's all that you have made.
Security and innerpeace
The gifts you've given me.
My heart, my love I give to you
With my promise I'll be forever true.

SHARON McCANN,
Long Eaton, Nottingham.

THE WONDER OF YOU

What a wonderful world we live in
With the Sun, the stars and the sky.
Where mountains sweep down to the ocean,
Snow-capped and wonderfully high.
Where rivers and streams gently idle
And glaciers melt in the sun,
Where the whole of creation is living
And the laughter of children such fun.
The Earth is alive with its magic
As crops emerge into view,
Drenching the land with such colour
No paint box could capture such hue.
Where did the birds get their colour?
The fish and the animals too?
Everything living is wonderful,
Especially the wonder of you.

MARY MONICA COOKSON,
Ribbleton, Preston, Lancashire.

A SUMMER'S DAY

Through golden fields our pathway lay
And far, far below, the shimmering bay,
Where like children pressed to a mother's breast
Lilliputian yachts lie at ease, at rest.
How naked they seem, their white wings still,
Like the gaunt lone pine on the headland hill,
    Yet like the pine, majestic still.
    Hand-in-hand we wend our way
    By paths bedecked with flowers,
    While up above, minstrel birds
    Charm the fleeting hours.
From every ledge on the beetling cliffs
    The seagulls plaintive cry
And wrapt in sunshine, summer seas
    Sing a gentle lullaby.
'Tis hard, hard to be sad on a day like this,
    When Mother Nature throws a kiss.
A kiss that's borne on the soft warm wings
Of the golden days, that summer brings.

RICHARD BUTWELL,
Kings Heath, Birmingham.

ON BEING ME

I am ME.
    I'm what you see
And that is what I'll always be,
    Just ME.
No matter what is done to me,
    I'll still be ME.
And though to some, I may be
    Really just a nobody,
There's no-one else I'd rather be
    Than ME.
All the trials in my life were meant to be
And despite these things I am content, you see
    Just
        Being
            ME.

FREDA LARTER,
Cherry Willingham, Lincoln.

THE DANCERS

The Flamenco dancers electrified the sultry night.
A flourish, a click and a whirl,
Castanets clicking, the audience in awe at the sight.
An Ole! From a beautiful girl,
Arms braced on hips, feet stamp upon the dusty floor.

Around one of the stage lights fireflies begin to dance,
Swooping in a frantic fatal flight.
They kiss the halo and others swirl for another chance
To waltz around the deadly light.
Wings crumpled, lifeless, they lie upon the dusty floor.

TERENCE J. BRADLEY,
South Yardley, Birmingham.

WILD OATS

My poems are my babies,
  often unplanned:
  suddenly a tiny seed runs wild -
      totally out of control, with a mind of its own -
      and the next thing I know it's a child,
      with a heart and a soul and a unique persona
      I can't re-arrange.

      Yet sometimes I long to:
      sometimes I feel I've been cheated
      of playing my part in their coming;
      sometimes I want to amend them
      and send them back to the beginning.
      But that's not an option
      and though I may find them imperfect
      or sadly deformed,
      sub-standard or handicapped,
      I've not the heart to deny them.
      Mother-love is innate:
      perhaps at the start I'd have taken
      some action, but that's when
      they raced off without me -
      and now that they're here
      it's too late.

My best babies always
  decide to be born in the bath,
    when I've nothing to write them on;
      and by the time I'm out and dry
        and ready for my active part,
          again it's too late ...
            for they're g
                  o
                n
              e
            .

CAROLYN KING,
Madeira Vale, Ventnor,
Isle of Wight.

TIM HENMAN

Loose-limbed and lithe,
He stretches wide
To play
An elegant
Cross-court forehand,
Timing the ball,
To perfection.

Tall, dark-haired,
And handsome,
He cuts a
Dashing figure,
Like the cartoon prince,
In a Disney film.

As the final backhand,
Goes wide,
He raises his arms
In triumph
To the crowd.
A champion, and,
A rare British treasure.

***KIRSTY-ANN WILKES,**
　　Kidderminster.

JUST GIRLS

Her father said she shouldn't mix with strangers.
He said life had such dangers held in store.
But she never really knew about those dangers
Until her country sent her off to war.

We need you girl, to make the ammunition
That feeds the hungry guns to shoot the Hun.
We need you girl, to work the ploughs and harrows,
That feed the hungry soldiers when they're done.

We need you girl, for typing up the orders,
We need your homely ways to make the beds.
To nurse our broken boys back to the front-line,
To wrap them up in clean sheets when they're dead.

And patronised she bore the idle chatter -
Just a typist, just a land-girl, just a nurse -
At work pretended that it didn't matter,
Though it made the weight of sacrifice feel worse.

Those orders may dispatch a troop to blazes,
But save a company from similar fate.
They sorted out insane from feigning crazies,
And requisitioned bully by the crate.

From circumstances less inclined to cattle,
Those land-girls wrought sibsistence from the earth.
They fought their own agrarian front-line battle -
Just a typist, just a land-girl, just a nurse.

Cattle trains stacked high with wounded soldiers,
Cattle stalls converted into berths,
Were scant defence against the strafing fighter,
Squirting tracer at the train for all he's worth.

And as the young girl faltered, then fell forward,
In one last dying duty, like her first,
She covered up her patient with her body.
Just a typist, just a land-girl, just a nurse.

ANDY TERRY,
Norton, Stoke-on-Trent.

REGRETS

I have strolled through splendid gardens
And dined in ornate rooms
Been etertained by hosts elite
Respected by their grooms
It didn't all come easily
I had to earn my place
And then I was a privileged one
Amid the human race
I married into money
And had a daughter fair
But at ten years old we lost her
That's when I ceased to care
It all seemed artificial
Why had I been so blind
Forgetting where my roots were
Leaving quality behind
I rarely saw my parents
Yet they'd given me my start
They never asked for royalties
It all came from the heart
And now I knew what loss was
I knew they had suffered too
I would give the world to make it up
If I could start anew.

MAUREEN TOOZE,
Great Barr, Birmingham.

MEMORIES AND DREAMS

Things can never be the same
Now that you have gone,
You've left me for that other world
And I'm still in this one.

The days and nights are lonely,
There's nothing more, it seems,
For all that I am left with
Are memories and dreams.

Memories of the happy times,
The laughter we once knew,
I can't imagine what life holds
In a future without you.

I know that when my time is up,
I'll climb that heavenly stair,
The pearly gates will open
And you'll be waiting there.

Once more we'll be together
Up in the sky so blue,
My wish will have been granted,
And I'll know that dreams come true.

FRANCES CHAMBERS,
Winterton, Scunthorpe.

ACCIDENTAL GIFT

My accident left my garden unattended,
   So the wild flowers I befriended.
To my surprise there was a joy,
   As no-one else did I employ
To clear the once offending weeds,
   So of course, they spread their seeds.
I now have a garden that does extend,
   A pleasure to many a wild friend.
There's Badger Bill who calls each night,
   He's gone before the morning light.
My feathered friends enjoy the seeds,
   Whilst Ladybirds feed off the weeds.
Butterflies display each day,
   Colours that are bright and gay.
Hedgehogs hide in a pile of leaves,
   Where the Ivy plant gently weaves
Its way unto a fallen apple tree,
   The chosen home of a Honey Bee.

My garden pond's another story,
   With Dragonflies in all their glory.
The Frogs are many, they return each year,
   Somedays a Heron will appear.
For his dinner he will steal the fish,
   It seems they make a tasty dish.
My garden now is so much pleasure,
   Red Poppies grow, beyond all measure.
Never again will I moan,
   When I see a weed has grown.
For I feel that God has given me,
   A valued gift and all for free ...

MARY I. MOUNTAIN,
Kenn, Exeter,
Devon.

THE INEVITABLE REVELATION

Slumbering in the embrace of a dear old comfy chair
With dusk's soft grey mantle spread around.
In a moment poised between dreams and earthly care
An awareness arose within to astonish and confound!
Shrouded in mysterious depths of oval splendour -
Mirrored across the firelight's flickering gloom,
A shadowy figure, with silver hair, looked out in silent scrutiny,
Eyes narrowed in assessment like my own.
Startled, my gaze wavered and withdrew its hidden plea.
Was this an apparition, an omen of dire immediacy?
An unspoken answer, caught between lip and cheek
Bubbled up as if to burst any mystery there to seek!
"Farewell, dear youth!" I bade in acknowledged recognition
(Quietly foregoing the loss of youthful aspiration!)
And accepting fate's inevitable toll for time's erosive passage,
Two silver heads bowed in a ghostly pre-destined marriage.
Now aquainted with the spectre on further retrospection
Laughter rang out to greet the mystical reflection;
Revealed! - A blythe semblance of my long departed mother
As she had been - as I am now - one within the other!

JOAN CORKILL,
Ramsey, Isle of Man.

WITH A LITTLE HELP

With a little help from my family of four,
There's often a little knock on my door.
They have to come to help me out
And leave behind a nice clean clout.

With a little help with my garden so bright,
A little help just keeps it right.
All it needs is loving care
To leave a space for me and my chair.

With a little help from my two old sticks,
They help me out from many a fix.
No longer are my legs agile,
I cannot even walk with style.

With a little help I can keep my home,
No longer do I long to roam.
With my eyes I still can see
And write about my family tree.

With a little help as time moves on,
My two sticks still help along;
But now that I am old and grey
There's nothing more for me to say.

With a little help, when my time has come,
Someone above will take me home.
My two old sticks will carry on
And help someone to walk along.

DAISY COOPER,
Kendal, Cumbria.

HALLOWEEN

A bright full moon shining in the sky,
Witches on their broomsticks flying high.
In their caves the cauldrons are steaming,
Being prepared for the plans they are scheming.
Eye of toad and wing of bat,
Then they add a nice fat rat,
Which was caught by their faithful black cat.

Their sorcery is working well,
As they stir up a magic evil spell.
Children with their faces painted
Roam the streets for trick or treat,
Throwing flour and water over others they meet.

It's a dark and foggy night,
As witches hatch up their darkest deeds.
It is a night for acting bold,
For evil things can happen, we are told;
And so many strange happenings will be seen,
For this is the night which is Halloween.

TERRI BRANT,
Pentwyn, Cardiff.

LETTING GO

I feel the approach of Autumn
and don't want to let go
of the warmth
and the glow
of summer.
It's slipping away, though.

The older I get
the more I regret its passing.
I mourn freedom bestowed
of eating outdoors,
of lying in sun,
of wearing my shorts
and taking long walks
at slow summer pace.

Will the joy of discovering
shy blue-black sloes
in prickly hedgerows,
and berries black ripe,
rose hips glowing bright
and crab apples small
on trees far too tall,
help to lessen the sadness I feel?

Diminishing days,
mornings shrouded in haze,
a nip in the air,
harvest moon hanging there,
familiar signs
fast approach,
and I *have* to let go
of the warmth
and the glow
of summer.

AUDREY HARDY,
Ratby, Leicester.

WHY?

Why does my Mum say No to me?
She says it all the time.
She never thinks it's her fault,
She always thinks it's mine.
It's "Don't do this"
Or "Don't do that",
And "No, No, NO"
All day,
She doesn't seem to understand that
I'm learning as I play.
I try so hard to please her
To do the things I should,
If she'd only say "No, don't BECAUSE ..."
I really think I could.
So come on Mum and let's be fair,
And I promise I will try,
To do the things you ask of me
But please do tell me why.

JANET STEVENSON,
Sprowston, Norwich.

CYCLE OF THE SEASONS
For Dionne, aged 5

Ruffled feathers huddle
from the breeze,
Shaking off nest-shyness
Fledglings nestle
in the branches of trees ...

GERALD ALDRED JUDGE,
New Mills, High Peak.

SILENT PLAYGROUND - VALE OF TEARS

There is a passage of a tear,
That trickles down Welsh vale,
Where angels watch over cradled bier,
Lulled by the song of nightingale ...

The hollow ring of a school-bell tolls,
And echoes through the vale,
While infants sleep in sweet repose,
Lulled by the song of nightingale ...

Light dwindles as a stream in summer,
A dusk-grey shroud ripples over vale,
'Neath conspiracy of cloud children slumber,
Lulled by the song of nightingale ...

GERALD ALDRED JUDGE,
New Mills, High Peak.

WINTER ELM

Majestically, you stand,
Cold and bare, but firm,
Grey are the skies you stretch up to,
Your roots in the frozen land.

How beautiful and warm you have been
On balmy summer days,
Clothed in leafy splendour,
Being your life long ways.

But, after winter cold has gone,
Your habit will return,
Whilst, I who stand and watch you,
For my kinsfolk yearn.

JUNE HUGHES,
Royston, Hertfordshire.

TOMORROW

Darkness is the curtain,
Drawn tight across my eyes.
With pinholes for the stars to shine,
In the evanescent skies.

Yet, nothing lasts forever,
Not sorrow, grief nor pain.
With the dawning of tomorrow,
The sun will shine again.

JOHN GRIFFITHS,
Solihull.

MEMORIES OF A MOMENT

I peered through the eye of a needle
And followed the thread mounted there,
It made patterns upon a tapestry.
It made pictures beautiful and dear.

A thread of silver to catch the sparkle
Of stars, upon your smile,
A thread of crystal as I hold your gaze
Just for a while.

Magnetic shades of gentle brown
Caress the colours of your glance,
And softened browns with jewels of gold,
As the sun and your hair dance.

Your skin was bathed in amber,
As you again turned your face to mine,
I felt the closeness of your breath.
Did you whisper, or did I?

You were embracing the fragrance of a tiny flower,
A deepest red evening rose,
And for a moment I lived in your smile,
Then gently, the eye of the needle closed.

LINDA RICHARDSON,
Kirby Frith, Leicester.

SCARECROWS

Scarecrows, a friendly type of being,
Round faces with a smile,
Home to tiny creatures,
Small birds to rest awhile.
Dressed in coat and hat, looking very smart,
Scarecrows stood so proud and straight,
They liked to look the part.
Have they all been made redundant,
Their work no longer needed?
Fluorescent boxes, flash and whirl,
Where new tilled earth, is seeded.
Have the scarecrows gone to Africa,
On some urgent kind of mission?
Are they there to help the starving poor,
Bring their crops to ripe fruition?
Or are they dying, in a cold wet ditch,
Forgotten, battered, torn,
No longer standing proudly,
To guard the growing corn?

ANNA BROOM,
Combs, Stowmarket,
Suffolk.

ONCE UPON A DREAM

Although my eyes no longer see
Your face is crystal clear
And though you're gone and not with me
Your voice is all I hear

My memories take me once more
Back to the home we shared
I feel again that love so sure
Knowing how you cared

Our cottage was our one delight
Our one and only home
The sunlit days and stars at night
We'd no desire to roam

Each table, chair and cooking pot
Was bought with loving care
You carved for me our baby's cot
And made a rocking chair

The years have passed but I can see
Each stick and every stone
I feel the joy that memory
Can bring, now I'm alone.

JACKIE JOHNSON,
Needham Market, Suffolk.

IN LOVING MEMORY OF A NAME

Weathered and worn
Loved and forlorn
Wrapped with mist on a sunlit dawn
Blanketed warmth with cherry blossom touch
So red, so white, so pink, so much
Infringing ragworts rise and rule
Dew collects in sparkling pools
Birdsong echoes and drifts by trees
Bent by restless gale and breeze
Monoliths of marble and slate
Carved with names
Etched with dates
Indistinct and bleached through age
Like ancient words on a parchment page
epithets dissolved by time
So destitute and so sublime
The church bell strikes to beckon the soul
To pay the piper
To honour the toll.

DAVID HARRISON,
Killingworth, Newcastle Upon Tyne.

ELECTRONIC EVOLUTION

Child is born with valves for heart
Dream of Babbage, child of Turing
Who would imagine this was the start?
Electronic Evolution about to begin

Soon came Mainframe, slave to man
Combining and counting in electric rage
Trying to combat as best it can
Tedious enslavement in metal cage

Then the light comes from the dark
Slowly the child talks to fellow machines
Transferring through its electric spark
Sharing its knowledge and its dreams

And as shared knowledge begins to grow
The child reacts with increasing speed
And man must feed its hunger to know
Slave to machine and his own greed

In clever moves it distorts reality
Virtual pleasure with no pain
Can man survive in this duality
Who has most to lose and most to gain?

In evolutionary cycle of the earth
Unwitting, but with guided hand
Man has enabled prescient birth
Sentient being now circles the land

In complex structure the network is linking
The creature has now escaped its cage
The earth is now alive and thinking
And so there dawns another age.

STEVE MESSENGER,
Balsham, Cambridge.

WINTER MAGIC

The mantle of winter snow 'neath sombre skies
    fades to grey as daylight dies.
Shadows close with groping fingers
    until no more the twilight lingers.
Now swirling clouds on winds of night
    reveal the hosts of stars so bright,
As glistening frost with silver sheen
    brings magic to the winter scene.

TOM CREAN,
Rednal, Worcestershire.

ONE MOMENT IN TIME

There was nothing special about the day.
    It was ordinary in every way,
Seated beneath an old tree
    Happy in Nature's company,
Not deep in thought,
    Rather, - content with idle musing,
Then quite unsought,
    There was an immensity of light,
As if the darkest night
    Had succumbed to a hundred brilliant suns,
And a timeless peace which gave increase
    To a certainty that past, present and future
Existences had no reality except as one,
    For one magnificent moment all was one
And then it was gone,
    One moment of exquisite rapture
I could never recapture.

FRED STARR,
Lowdham, Nottinghamshire.

SOUTHAMPTON WATER

A breath of fresh air, a stroll along the Solent
I sit here and pause on this bench for a moment
A picturesque scene of yachts and ships sailing
And the seagulls above gently gliding and wailing

The sun as it sets in the warmth of the evening
The cruise liner looks so serene as it's leaving
As passengers wave from the deck of its stern
Heading for warmer climes which they yearn

But a glance to the left is a sight for sore eyes
Black smoke spewing into the evening skies
From a place by night and day men they do toil
To produce for our use all those barrels of oil

A blot on the landscape - a grim sight by day
But by night takes on quite a different array
With lights that can be seen from far and wide
It's funny that by night it can look quite "refined"

The sea looks so cold as it laps on the shore
A cluster of pebbles, seaweed and more
The mess of the litter of cans and waste paper
It's all washed up now - but will go out again later

It's all sort of things from beginning to end
The grey dismal docks - just around the bend
The yachts at full sail - all shimmering and clean
But for me it's a place I just come here to dream.

AMANDA C. COMPTON,
Southampton.

LAVINIA

Such sweet joy thy nearness brings
    perfumed like a breath of spring,
Filling each day with endless pleasure,
    recalling dreams of youth to treasure
And though the years saw many trials,
    each were met with love and smiles.
So now my love, with all my heart
    I pledge to thee we'll never part.

TOM CREAN,
Rednal, Worcestershire.

JUDGEMENT DAY

Life is a stairway to Heaven,
Each step must be trodden with care,
One step at a time, till we get to the top,
Taking the just, with the unfair.
Listening and learning, life can be hard,
Look over your shoulder, be on your guard,
Saying you're sorry, when you know you are wrong,
Keeping a promise, to help you feel strong,
Helping the aged needy and weak,
For these are the ones, that life can be bleak,
If I can do all these tasks I've been given,
I'll feel that my life was really worth living.
When I reach the top step
I'll stand there and wait,
For someone to open that big pearly gate.

MARCIA LUXON,
Exeter, Devon.

A PERFECT DAY

Thunder booming, darkness looming,
Hangs heavily in the humid air.
Your coffin lowered reluctantly into the ground.
All that remains, a sunken mound.

The gods are angered and
Cascading rivulets of tears shed,
As they take your hand and you're led
To the comfort and safety of Heaven's bed.

Those that are left on this mortal earth
Mutely mourn your loss, await rebirth.
The time for reconciliation will come
And all with open arms will welcome you home.

All, we knew this day would come,
When earth and you would unite, become one.
When come what come may, the end,
The ghastly end would come, to this a perfect day.

JOANNA MOORE,
Norwich, Norfolk.

THE BLACK-HOODED CROW

Nature's Pirate

Loud raucous bird, black-cloaked with razor beak,
Circling in gathered flight around tree-top domain
So crude and perilously balanced on branches bleak;
Laughing maniacally with loud, harsh throaty cry -
Nature's undertaker, who feeds on those who die.

A black-feathered pirate, sombre and over-bearing,
Cruel hooded eyes glistening with satanic malice
In early morning sun, or evening's rays fast fading;
Or strutting by wayside verge to tarmacadam clean
And dormant remnants of foul carrion to glean.

Cruel scavenger bird, whose hunger cannot be sated;
Who steals from nests or takes proud ewe's young kin
And plunders souls of siblings; you are verily hated
By all who see your black shadow encircling the trees,
And lofting o'er hedgerows into valley's sheltered lea.

MICHAEL K. MOORE,
Norwich, Norfolk.

INVOY (Message)

Evolved, by Time's slow catalyst,
    (we think, therefore we are), insist
    we speak, we feel, we love; accept
    t'was neither wit nor conscience kept
    when pristine man first woman kissed.

Turn, ustulate-skeined galaxy,
    (mused halcyon-blest Calliope);
    should'st dreamers, or 'sad-atomed jars',
    ponder two hundred billion stars
    nigh nepheline-shored arcane sea?

Why, unto fardel-trammeled care
    such heedless minds would'st waken; there,
    from wrong thoughts cast, (dire words reveal),
    through actions past, fell fate shall seal
    'twixt sigh-lent scream and fervent prayer.

Self, fortune-changer of soul state,
    causeth thy path, set incarnate;
    (those ego hastes put much awry).
    Could'st thou avoid thy clown called "I",
    thy destiny ameliorate!

Might artful-faced caporifact,
    from one's id-entity detract?
    Whose image-subterfuge, opaque,
    faults Spirit's scan on his mistake?
    Think'st, fool, thy God will not exact?

Writ, blazon'd deep in runic gold,
    (Memory's daughter's gift, untold),
    'courage'; we cope with then - here - now,
    while life-pursuing who?, what?, how?,
    new former-future hope to hold.

MICHAEL ROY,
Southampton.

Continued ...

KEY TO 'INVOY (Message)

Calliope: Ancient Greek diety of epic poetry.

Sad-atomed jar: ref. Lord Byron (1788-1824).

Caporifact: Author's coined word for *a head through hole, senic-flat, photographic device.*

ref. Latin *Cappo* (head); *Oris* (hole); and *Factum* (something made).

THE HILTON HOUSE ANTHOLOGY SERIES

Hilton House (Publishers) was introduced to specialise and establish interest in British poetry by giving writers of verse the opportunity of having their poetry appreciated, printed and publicised.

The anthologies published are carefully arranged with all copy preparation and type-setting carried out in-house by qualified staff, using the latest Desk Top Publisher aids. All poems in Hilton House publications are centralised and left justified on each page, unless directed otherwise by the author. Great care is taken in page layout and each book is printed in A5 softback or hardback format with designed cover and with pages printed on good quality paper.

Authors may also submit their poems for general anthology selection. It would be appreciated if a SAE is enclosed with your introductory letter.

To aspire confidence in poets, two national competitions are held each year, open to authors throughout the British Isles. The first of these is held from January 2nd to March 31st (The Hilton House National Poet of the Year Competition). Cash prizes are available for the first eighteen places and certificates of Special Commendation are awarded to all poets short-listed in the final selections. The second competition is held from July 2nd to August 31st (The Hilton House National Open Competition). Cash prizes are available for the first three places and all poets selected for publication are awarded certificates of Special Commendation. Rules and conditions of entry for both competitions can be obtained on receipt of a SAE.

Membership of the Fraternity of Poets is by invitation only.

Further information can be obtained by writing, or telephoning:

> **Hilton House (Publishers),
> Hilton House, 39 Long John Hill,
> Norwich, Norfolk NR1 2JP.**
>
> *Tel: (01603) 449845*

(Also in the Hilton House Poetry Anthology Series)

POETIC INSPIRATIONS.

REFLECTIONS
(featuring poems by: Alene Kimm, Ceri Harwood and Gerald Aldred Judge)

IMAGES OF THOUGHT
(featuring poems by: Margaret Solly, Michael Roy and Dennis F. Tye).

THE FLOWERS OF THE FOREST ...
A Dedication to British and Commonwealth War Dead
(An Anthology of Poetry and Historical Notes)

Other Works
(Reference and Military History)
by Michael K. Moore

BATTALION AT WAR - SINGAPORE 1942.
(Published by Gliddon Books)

HILTON HOUSE
IS A MEMBER OF THE POETRY SOCIETY
AND